CONTENT

AF282487

Europe

Lost her Sovereignty

History – Background - Perspectives

by

Georg von Goldbach

This book is a revised version of
Part Three and a part of the Epilogue of the
book

Europe on the Way to her Apocalypse

History – Background – Perspectives

Bibliographic information from the German National Library:
The German National Library lists this publication in the German National Bibliography; detailed bibliographic data are available online at https://dnb.de.

© 2024, Georg von Goldbach
Verlag: BoD • Books on Demand GmbH, In de Tarpen 42, 22848 Norderstedt
Druck: Libri Plureos GmbH, Friedensallee 273, 22763 Hamburg
ISBN: 978-3-7597-7663-1

This book cannot say anything about whether and how humanity will solve her problems... It can only convey how little we know...

It can also confirm what many have known for a long time, namely that historiography .. is the record of the crimes and madness of humanity. It is no help for prophecies.

The Age of Extremes, World History of the 20th Century
Century
Eric Hobsbawm

Foreword to the book

The personal motivation for this book comes from my realization that the creation of peace is, in our time, the most important concern of humanity. I was born in Germany and can therefore say that war is in my blood, as it is the case for most Europeans. A great number of wars have been waged on European ground among the European nations over the past centuries. In response to that, the European Union has been created and has progressively been shaped after the End of the Second World War as a "peace project".

This hope is waning more and more, and Europe does not seem capable of escaping the claws of the evil of war.

In the decades after 1993, I had increasingly worked as a consultant for the European Union (EU). In the beginning, I was very happy and even enthusiastic to do this, as long as the EU's credible intention for "international partnership" was still the guiding principle for the work of our advisory services and activities abroad. After 2001, however, I had noticed how an intentional effort for dominance had increasingly come to the fore within the foreign policy of the EU. Relations with partner countries became increasingly political, less characterized by friendship and the honest dealings among partners. Of course, this change in attitude had also become obvious to many of our partners in the countries in which we worked. I am more of a free and liberal spirit by nature, and ideological narrow-mindedness has never been one of my personal traits. However, I have always endeavored to consciously guide my actions based on my ethical convictions and moral principles.

I can say that peaceful development among people and nations based on shared values and principles has always been a matter close to my heart. That is why I didn't feel challenged in particular when I was asked to consciously and with conviction, but without personal zeal or even fanaticism, to work for the healthy development of Europe and its relations with other countries in the world. My anxiety therefore increased more and more as certain authoritarian tendencies in the EU and the European Commission became more frequently apparent to me. I then drafted an essay in 2017, essentially for myself, to clearly articulate my own thoughts, entitled "How Europe Lost Her Sovereignty". In it, I showed how, in the interplay between Germany and France, which had become a second spiritual home for me, the European Commission usurped the sovereignty of the nation states and increasingly restricted their national responsibility. In addition, as a "participating observer", I had recognized that a war was being prepared on European soil. Of course, that was not easy to see at the time. All the friends, acquaintances and business partners I wanted to point out only looked into the air when I talked about it.

Nobody wanted to know anything about it. I myself did not investigate this question and, of course, could not know in what form this war would then begin and take place. I was also personally surprised by the way, with a flick of the wrist, Germany and Europe were driven into this war, which was foreseeable by 2014 at the latest and then turned into an open war in 2022.

Personally, this experience has shaken me very much, also in my trust in people as a whole. I didn't want to believe how sensible and intelligent people could get involved in such stupidity. The experience of this irrationality still pains me very much. My grandfather was sent into the First World War in 1914 with the motto "Cannon thunder is our greeting". My father went to war in 1939 for the Hitler regime, from which he was not to return home from Russian captivity until the end of 1947[1], severely damaged in

---

[1] At a time when Russia is once again under strong ideological attack, it is necessary to confess that I have not developed any negative attitude or resentment from my father's experience in the mines of Russia. My father had been a prisoner of war (Kgf) and his imprisonment was therefore the result of a war that had arisen and been waged in a criminal way.

physical health and also mentally. And now, at the end of my life, the war was to haunt me and perhaps plague my children as well.

I have always consciously enjoyed and never despised the great fortune of growing up in peace and being able to shape my life peacefully. Peace had always seemed to me to be a great and precious good that had to be carefully preserved. Unfortunately, we did not succeed in this.

Chapter 1

The spiritual fathers of this book

The intellectual authorship of this book is held by two American thinkers and visionaries. The two have never met in person, but what they have in common is that they derive their thinking from cybernetics as a scientific means to understand and explain our world[2]. This is obvious in the case of Gregory Bateson[3], because he speaks of it

---

[2] Cybernetics is the science of controlling anc regulating machines in analogy to the functioning of living organisms by means of feedback processes that receive impulses from the sense organs. In social organizations, feedback works through information, communication and participant observation. The science of cybernetics was born from the cooperation of scientists in the "Vienna Circle". It was formulated by Norbert Wiener after 1945, after his emigration to the USA, when he came to the realization that intelligent behavior can be described as the result of feedback mechanisms.

[3] In the case of Gregory Bateson, we are essentially referring to the collection of essays published as "Ecology of the Mind" in 1985. The English edition of "Steps to an Ecology of Mind, Collected Essays" dates from 1972.

frequently in his writings. In the case of R. Buckminster Fuller[4], the reference to cybernetics is visible everywhere in his writings and also in his works, but he was more of a pragmatist and generalist nature. "Bucky" Fuller strove to live a life, in which he fought for the practical implementation of his ideas, mainly through the use and application of his design artifacts, while Gregory Bateson limited himself to theoretical and epistemological reflection and teaching.

What they both have in common is that they were very sharp observers of what was going on in the world and were always keen to understand how people acted. Both have always put people at the center of their efforts and have always looked at people in a larger, more comprehensive context and from a system view. In Buckminster Fuller's case, it was "man in the universe." For

---

[4] At Buckminster Fuller, our main source is his book "Critical Path", which was published in 1981. Probably his best-known book is "Operating Manual for Spaceship Earth", from 1969. It can be downloaded online from the Buckminster Fuller Institute website. The German edition of "Instruction Manual for the Spaceship Earth and Other Writings" dates from 2011.

Gregory Bateson, a trained anthropologist and biologist, it was the systemic relation between man and nature. What both have in common is that they saw the fundamental fallacy in human thought and action in the fact that man saw himself disconnected from these necessary systemic relations with nature and the universe. Both explained this as the result of the one-sided emphasis on the development of the natural sciences since the 17th century, which has led to a mechanistic world view. This paradigm of human isolation from nature and the universe, as both saw it, has slowly dissolved again since the early 20th century with quantum mechanics and new insights gained by biology in the self-regulating systems of life. These scientific discoveries generated progressively a new world view that related life and the role of humanity to the "uncertainty principle". A door into the unknown had opened. From now on, the meaning of life and human nature were perceived in a new light. It had become possible to reconnect with the nature of man and his importance in the cosmos.[5]

---

[5] Fritjof Capra gives a catchy account of this in his "Tao of Physics", of 1977.

This sums up the experience shared by Gregory Bateson and Buckminster Fuller.

In order to understand these two great minds, we would like to emphasize the decisive basic idea that is characteristic of each of them. Buckminster Fuller developed his fundamental ideas after 1930, formulated them in 1969 in his *Operating Manual for Spaceship Earth,* and summarized them with the formulation of *Synergetics* as *Explorations into the Geometry of Thinking*[6]. Intuitively, he seized the need for the application of "general principles and laws" to the understanding of the functioning of *Man in Universe*. He convincingly shows that it is not a lack of energy that inhibits the development of humanity. Rather, the fundamental mistake lies in the fact that humanity has not found, not understood, the access to the infinite source of energy that is provided to us from the universe through the sun. This lack of access to understanding eternally regenerating energy has so far kept people caught in a self-made trap. According to Buckminster Fuller, this phenomenon can be

---

[6] This is the title of a book first published in 1975, in cooperation with E. J. Applewhite.

traced back to the work of British economist Thomas Robert Malthus, who established at the beginning of the 19th century the principle that humans would reproduce with the necessary fatefulness, but at the same time had only limited natural resources at their disposal. Hence, the fight for limited resources was inevitable. For Darwin, this became the struggle for existence and led Darwinists to formulate the principle of "survival of the fittest". If we take these thoughts just a few steps further, we end up directly at the rationale for the demand for "unlimited growth" of the economy, and at the political level, for the hegemonic striving and the seemingly inevitable wars as a means of gaining power, which are at the center of the critical analysis of our book.

Gregory Bateson is an anthropologist and a biologist by training. He has also worked successfully in psychology and psychiatry[7]. However, he has the most important significance as a researcher on epistemology, and in particular on the importance of

---

[7] The term "double-bind", i.e. the relationship trap, was coined by him.

cybernetics for the sciences and for the shaping of human living conditions on earth.

He says of himself that "the two most important historical events in my life were the Treaty of Versailles and the discovery of cybernetics".[8] This certainly sounds astonishing, because it is not immediately clear what the relationship between these two "events" looks like. We come closer to understanding what Gregory Bateson means when he says that, in his view, the "important question for history is: has the default[9] or attitude been changed?". He goes on to explain that "the most important points in history are... the historical moments... in which attitudes are changed", in which previous "values" change. He then shows that the Treaty of Versailles has not successfully changed the attitudes and values of the most

---

[8] In this part, we essentially refer to Gregory Bateson, "Ecology of the Mind, Part VI, Crises in the Ecology of the Mind, from Versailles to Cybernetics", from his lecture in 1966.

[9] The term "specification" here refers to cybernetics, as a system theory, and means "leadership variable" or "decisive reference value" to which the other parameters and elements of a system are oriented.

important signatories of the treaty[10], i.e. Germany, France, Great Britain and the USA.[11] Therefore, according to his understanding, the inevitable consequence of the Treaty of Versailles was the Second World War, with the same nations as important protagonists. He calls the Treaty of Versailles one of the "greatest relapses in the history of our civilization" and says that "we will have to deal with the aftermath of this betrayal for a number of generations to come", before adding that "betrayal in an armistice or in peace negotiations is worse than a stratagem in battle." His conclusion: "It goes on and on. The tragedy of fluctuating, self-propagating mistrust, hatred and destruction through generations".

---

[10] We should note here that since the October Revolution of 1917, a government had taken power in Russia with which the United States did not want to come to an understanding.

[11] As we will show later, it was precisely this thought that guided Rudolf Steiner in his assessment of the events surrounding the First World War. He insisted that it was necessary to change the political "rules" in order not to prepare a new catastrophe. As we know, Max von Baden, the last Reich Chancellor of the German Empire, very soon ended Rudolf Steiner's advisory activities.

Gregory Bateson is aware that cybernetics, i.e. "the second historical event" of his time, will not in itself bring the solution to our geopolitical problems. But he sees that it can be a contribution to changing attitudes and behavior. But he also knows that "any understanding can be used destructively". He summarizes his insight as follows: "In cybernetics itself there is integrity[12], which helps us not to be seduced by it into another madness, but we cannot trust that it will keep us from sin"[13] and then he adds in a more hopeful tone: "But this much is certain, that in cybernetics there is also the means to achieve a new and perhaps human worldview, a means to change our philosophy of power and a means to see our own stupidities in a larger perspective".

---

[12] Because cybernetics allows us to see the connections between events.
[13] We would like to note here that Buckminster Fuller also sees integrity as a very important criterion for good and successful action. That's how he called one of his books, "Ideas and Integrities", from 1963. He also emphasizes this point in his "Critical Path".

Chapter 2

The European Policy Framework

Just a decade ago, we would have said that the intention we pursued with our book was to prevent Europe from being drawn into a new war, or being driven into it. Today, at the beginning of 2024, as we write this introduction, we will be too late with this appeal against war. Europe has entered into an open war again since 2022. This is not a "Cold War", as it is still offered to the public by the media. Since February 2022, probably close to one million soldiers and civilians have already died in this war. Millions are on the move and fleeing the war zone and its borderlands.

How could this happen? Cynically, one could answer: because the 14,000 Russian-speaking residents in the Luhansk and Donetsk regions, killed in their own country by the Ukrainian government since 2014, after the "Euro-Maidan", were not counted. In German, they say that they "did not count", i.e. they were not worth counting. Cynical? It's wartime again!

Behind this concealment of the terrorization and killing of its own population by the Ukrainian government, however, there was intention, one may assume "bad intention".

In 2015, the Minsk Agreement was signed in a binding manner under international law, and Germany, France, Russia and Ukraine pretended to take responsibility for its implementation. The main focus was on the observance of a ceasefire and the negotiation of an autonomous status for the two Russian-speaking regions of Luhansk and Donetsk.

However, as it turned out, there was no manifest intention on the part of Ukraine and the Western states that had signed the Minsk agreement to implement this agreement. As former Chancellor Angela Merkel publicly stated in 2023, the main intention of the Minsk agreement was to "buy Ukraine time"[14]. Since 2015, Ukraine has been massively armed by NATO to prepare for an imminent war with Russia. That had been the

---

[14] As an example from the Tagesspiegel of 09.12.2022, where it says: "The former Chancellor described the "Minsk Peace Agreement" of 2014 as an attempt to give Ukraine time.

intention behind the staging of the Euro Maidan. In order to spread fog and give Russia hope, in the years from 2018 to 2020, new fragile ceasefire agreements were reached on average every three months by the Trilateral Contact Group for Ukraine, consisting of Russia, Ukraine and the OSCE[15].

Today, it is obvious that NATO's preparations for a war with Russia have been in full swing since 2015 at the latest. The Ukrainian army has been massively upgraded and supported by European and American military advisers.

Russia put an end to this false and nasty game in February 2022, with its attack on Ukraine. In terms of its own self-defense, Russia found herself in a situation, in which the country had no other choice.

---

[15] OSCE stands for the Organization for Security and Co-operation in Europe. The OSCE emerged as an international institution from the negotiations on "Security and Co-operation in Europe", which ended in 1975 with the Helsinki Final Act. We cite this to show that 50 years ago, there was a will for peaceful cooperation in Europe. This initiative has been completely destroyed since 1990, with the end of the Soviet Union. The will to war has regained the upper hand.

What can be achieved with this book in such a situation? Why do we address it to the public?

The crucial question we want to ask ourselves is: what were the reasons for the sabotage of the Minsk agreement by the Western powers and NATO? What were the intentions behind the preparation of the war against Russia? After all, as we will see in detail, Germany and France were only proxies for the "global West", i.e. for NATO, in this tactical game.

Methodologically, we want to advance from the perception of symptoms to the understanding of reality in order to answer this question. The answer to our questions is hidden behind the veil of symptoms[16] that only show us a semblance of reality through false mirror images of reality that want to fool us. The most important instrument we will apply for understanding reality will be thinking, and the most important prerequisite is our own fearlessness in order to face the

---

[16] In his lectures of 1919 on the symptomatology of history, Rudolf Steiner challenges us to see the reality behind the symptoms, the truth behind the events. S. h. the lectures in GA 185:
https://anthrowiki.at/Geschichtliche_Symptomatologi e.

often terrible (un)truths and lies, for which some of our fellow humans are responsible. If we courageously face reality in this sense, then we will increasingly come to an understanding of the "spiritual driving forces" that are effective behind the behavior of some of the key political and economic actors behind the veil. In the course of our analytical description, we will provide important insights into these processes of geopolitics and the striving for global hegemonial power that is going on behind the veil.

For those who want to face reality, the facts are not so difficult to understand. Of course, one must be willing not to be blinded, not to be satisfied with the "colored reflections"[17] of reality, that the media and our political leaders are spreading everywhere.

Intelligent and honest political analysts, such as Noam Chomsky, have been telling us what is going on behind the veil for decades. In an interview in the *New Left Review* (No. 57, September/October 1969), which was published in Germany in the appendix

---

[17] A winged saying that Goethe puts into the mouth of his Faust; see Faust II, Act One.

Linguistics and Politics to the book *Language and Spirit*, Chomsky said: "The goal of creating an integrated world economy dominated by American capital ranks first for the elite that governs the United States. It's not just about having safe areas for American investment, markets, and control over raw materials, as important as they may be. It is also necessary to keep defense-spending, i.e. ultimately the costs of war, at a high level. This is the most important Keynesian mechanism for maintaining what is called a healthy economy". This is a clear statement: high spending on a war economy is seen by US power elites as an important mechanism for maintaining a healthy economy. We will have to come back to this point when we talk about the war economy, into which the EU and her various member states have been forced since 2023 by the hegemonial policies of the USA. As Eckart Conze writes: "Research rightly and almost unanimously considers the USA to be the hegemonic power of the Western world since 1945"[18].

---

[18] Eckart Conze; Hegemonie durch Integration: Die amerikanische Europapolitik und ihre Herausforderung durch de Gaulle, in: Institute für Zeitgeschichte,

By taking away the veil that is covering the reality behind the symptoms, their historical origin and their connections, we want to show a way to come to an in-depth understanding of important political and economic processes and contexts in our time. This kind of "analytical and symptomatologic history" should then provide the basis for making a diagnosis, which we see as a prerequisite for showing possible future solutions to eventually eliminate the root causes of the evils we have identified.

With our symptomatologic look at history, we pretend not to remain at the symptomatic level with the analysis we are undertaking, but we intend to explore this question of reasons and intentions behind the veil of historical symptoms. In this, we want to shed light on the reality of events and processes from different angles and aspects in order to understand how Europe got on the path to its self-destruction and its imminent apocalypse. At the end of this analytical and intellectual process we will go through in this book, it should become clear what the situation in

Vierteljahreshefte für Zeitgeschichte, Jahrgang 43 (1995), Heft 2.

Europe is today and where the path taken will consequently lead in the coming years and decades. It should have become obvious that we don't want to write war reportage, nor do we want to indulge in the diplomatic backstabbing in detail, as it has been and still is presented in the media every hour for years now. Our goal is to come to an understanding of the deeper reasons and drivers of these processes that currently shape our lives in Europe.

We also do not intend to write a comprehensive scientific treatise, in which the relationships and interdependencies of politics, economics and society are explained in detail. Rather, we are concerned with creating evidence for the driving forces and connections behind the events and facts that are becoming more and more obvious. Following this line of reasoning also requires the courage to face the facts and not to be afraid of the consequences of an impending catastrophe, towards which we are heading with our eyes wide open. It is our conviction that this catastrophe can no longer be prevented. In mid-2024, we are already moving into its very center. Europe is rapidly heading toward its own apocalypse at a breathtaking pace in a dynamic process of self-destruction.[19]

Through our academic research on history and political economy, we have learned that there are forces at work in history, good and bad, that cannot always be precisely named and do not follow any "logic". That is what the historian Eric Hobsbawm is hinting at in his pessimistic words, which we have quoted on top of this book. We wanted to take this insight from Eric Hobsbawm as a starting point, not as our final conclusion. In our book, we will also repeatedly give references to benevolent actors and good forces, who are trying to counteract this impending European catastrophe. As long as these actors and forces exist, we should not give up hope completely.

---

[19] We are not the first or the only ones to have come to such an understanding. Emmanuel Todd, who has published several books on the subject, is one of the examples. Available in German are: World Power USA: An Obituary, from 2003; available in French: La Défaite de l'Occident, from 2024. However, we have developed our own line of argumentation that starts from historical processes in order to then argue consistently in the sense of political economy.

However, our thesis will be that Europe and the so-called "West" will find it very difficult to find their way out of this catastrophe on their own.

In our Epilogue to this book, we will finally provide a concrete indication of the first and decisive step towards a geopolitical paradigm shift that can lead Europe out of this imminent apocalypse.

With this book, we will limit ourselves to the period of the past century. These have been the decisive one hundred years for this path to catastrophe that Europe has traveled. So we start in the time shortly before the First World War, when Diaghilev and Stravinsky staged their "Ballet Russe" and "Le Sacre du Printemps" (the "Rites of Spring") in Paris, when Oswald Spengler published the first drafts for his "Downfall of the West", when Thomas Mann wrote his "Death in Venice" and was inspired to write his "Magic Mountain", and when C. G. Jung had his visions of the blood flowing all over the European continent.[20]

In an overview, we will show what the "World after Versailles", i.e. after the threshold year of 1919, looked like and what perspectives were created by the political leaders for this world after the "primordial catastrophe" of the First World War. In doing so, we will gain insights into the process, in which the USA[21] entered the political and economic world stage as the decisive actor for Europe and the West.

In a further step, we will then trace the process how "Europe lost Her Sovereignty". This process and its outcome may be considered one of the most important events in European history since the French Revolution. We will show that the process of

---

[20] It is worth reading the 1989 book "Rites of Spring: The Great War and the Birth of the Modern Age", by the Latvian-Canadian historian Modris Eksteins.
[21] We limit our overview largely to Europe. We do not want to write a history of American global politics here. Our primary concern is to show the effects of the hegemonic policy of the USA on the weal and woes of Europe. However, as we will see, this hegemonic global politics naturally has its effects on the rest of the world as well.

European unification after 1945, which the whole world has followed with great respect and hope, has not resulted in the hoped-for liberation from the shackles of the past. Europe has not become an ambassador of peace in a multipolar world, as it seemed possible after 1957[22] and again after 1990. Rather, we will have to understand how Europe gradually abandoned itself and tied its fate directly to that of the USA and NATO, in particular after the event of 9/11, 2001. From a political point of view, this abandonment of the European sovereignty was probably the most important result of the Second World War. The former great European powers, England, France, Italy and Germany, had become vassals of the USA[23]. Already out of the "primordial catastrophe" of the First World War, Europe has become permanently and directly dependent on the USA. The former European great powers have degenerated into vassals of American

---

[22] Conclusion of the Treaty of Rome, establishing the EEC.
[23] See Zbigniew Brzeziński, The Grand Chessboard.

imperialism and American hegemonic politics[24].

In this introduction, we also want to point out an important issue that is usually ignored or concealed in the literature on the subject of "American hegemony". This concerns the economic and financial situation of the USA and the dominance of the dollar as an international means of payment.[25] The Bretton Woods system was fundamentally built on the gold standard. In 1971, at a time when the U.S. had a large and growing financing need for its war in Vietnam, then-U.S. President Richard Nixon removed the dollar's peg to gold in order to completely liberalize exchange rates in 1973. This was the beginning of a creeping process in which the US's trading partners, warned by the growing US debt, gradually lost their trust in the US. A

---

[24] This policy of American imperialism and American hegemonic politics is described and understood in great detail and plausibly by Niall Ferguson in his 2004 book "Colossus: The Rise and Fall of the American Empire".

[25] On this, Fundamentals of Monetary Foreign Trade, 2009, Gerhard Rübel.

process that has steadily intensified until our time.

For decades, at the latest with the "bursting of the tech bubble"[26] around the year 2000 and then with the "bursting of the real estate bubble" that led to the "Lehmann crisis" of 2008[27], the global financial crisis had become obvious as a systemic problem of US-Hegemony. These financial crises have been largely driven by US fiscal policy. They were caused by two main factors: an extremely expansive monetary policy (keyword: "helicopter money") promoted by the FED (the so-called "Federal Reserve System" of the USA), and the gigantic growth of financial resources and the related financial and economic power of the global financial cartels, such as "Black Rock"[28]. Europe also experienced its own financial crisis, the so-

---

[26] In the boom phase of the "New Economy" between 1995 and 2000, the number and capital strength of these new technology companies on the international stock exchanges increased rapidly.

[27] The bankruptcy of the investment bank Lehman Brothers on September 15, 2008, triggered a global financial crisis.

[28] An infinite source of information on this: https://de.wikipedia.org/wiki/BlackRock

called Euro-crisis. However, it was "solved" in a way that increased the dependence on the financial and economic policies of the USA and its global financial cartels. A large part of European companies and the remaining economic and financial capacities of Europe, which had not yet been in the hands of the USA and its financial cartels, were amicably helped out of the crisis by the USA. They were supported financially by the USA, which means "bought up", and robbed of their previous economic independence.

These are all topics that have been much discussed and also dealt with by journalists and scientists. We do not want to retake these discussions here. Rather, we are interested in showing the situation, in which Europe has found herself since then. In doing so, it is important for us to point out the mechanisms that the United States are knowingly and strategically implementing in order to achieve the goals of its imperialist hegemonic policy. As we know, these mechanisms for managing geopolitical regions and spheres have been tested by the United States essentially in the geopolitical region of the Middle East, having taken over the role of the British Empire there after the First World War. This region is home to the so-called "Arab" states, which, after the First World War, primarily took on the role of oil and energy suppliers for the world economy[29]. In our book on "War and Business: The American Success Story of the Past Century," published in 2024, we have shown in detail how these mechanisms, which were developed by the USA in the Arab region, have now given rise to the Business Model of the American foreign and hegemonic policy in an act of deployment of the political strategy.

We want to conclude this part of the book with references to the new role that the USA has assigned to the states of Europe. Consistent in its hegemonic and imperialist endeavors, the US demands that the European states, now also directly through their influence in the EU, play their role as exclusive partners of the USA. Since 2022, this role has also included a shift to an authoritarian war economy via the NATO

---

[29] Information on this is available at:
https://de.wikipedia.org/wiki/Organisation_erd%C3%B6lexportierender_L%C3%A4nder.

mechanism, together with a readiness to wage proxy wars for NATO and the USA, as we are currently experiencing in Ukraine. Europe's sovereignty has therefore been completely suspended. Europe, as an entire continent, has become a vassal of the United States.

We would like to elaborate at least briefly on a particularly critical factor in these mechanisms and processes at the end of this introduction. We have already briefly pointed out the decisive effect of the US debt. The key point is that the level and volume of U.S. debt are not sustainable. [30] The point we want to make here is relatively simple and direct. It is taken from the wisdom of all great cultures

---

[30] We refer here once again to Niall Ferguson, who, at the end of his book "Colossus: The Rise and Fall of the American Empire", asks the question of why American imperialism, which he has a rather positive attitude towards on the whole, will ultimately fail. Niall Ferguson has devoted himself to two main themes in his books: war and financing. His clear statement: the USA will fail due to over-indebtedness, i.e. a f nancing crisis.
On the subject of the over-indebtedness of the USA, we refer to numerous studies that have been written by economists and financial experts of all circles and backgrounds in recent decades on this topic.

and can be found in every good manual of political economy[31]. The question is: What can, and will the USA do to get out of this extreme debt? Inflation will no longer be enough, the flood of money over the past decades has been too great for that. So there is only one remedy: going to war. War as "creative destruction", [32]as a way out of the

---

[31] A recent Mises Institute podcast said, "They'll Never Pay Down the National Debt," meaning that "the Fed will never repay its debt. Instead, the Fed has two options: galloping inflation or insolvency.
However, we see a third option that is currently unfolding on a global scale: WAR.
In economics, this is called "capital destruction", i.e. setting all counters to zero and starting the show all over again, albeit at a higher level.
On this, see Friedrich A. v. Hayek, Weltwirtschaftliches Archiv, Vol. 36 (1932); pp. 86-108 (23 pages); and also in Ludwig von Mises, in his explanations of the processes in times of depression, as can be read in his theory of business cycles, which he presented in his work "Theory of Money and Means of Circulation", published in 1912.
[32] We borrow the term "creative destruction" from the Austrian economist Joseph Alois Schumpeter, who coined it in his theory of macroeconomics to characterize entrepreneurial performance through innovation and creative adaptation. For our purposes,

over-accumulation of capital. We just quote one article on this subject, which is from the magazine *Luxembourg*: Another crisis?[33]. There it is written about Europe, with reference to the "Great Depression" of 1873: "It sought a way out in rearmament, imperialism and finally in the First World War".

And it is indeed the case that the USA has already gone down this path again and will follow it even more intensively in the future as its debt increases. At the same time, Europe, also heavily and increasingly indebted, will once again have to go to war. Since 2022, there has been open talk of a war economy in the important countries of Europe and by the European Commission. The war economy is the future, towards which the European economies and societies are heading[34]. As early as 2023, the

---

we take the term broader and combine it with the concept of the overaccumulation of capital.

[33] Luxemburg, Zeitschrift für Gesellschaftskritik and Linke Praxis. https://zeitschrift-luxemburg.de/artikel/wieder-einmal-eine-krise/

[34] To be read in the Handelsblatt of 11.03.2023: Macron sees his country in the "war economy" - arms companies benefit. The German Defense Minister has

corresponding "turning point" has been defined as inevitable by the EU and several important member states. The development of the states of Europe is now rigorously dictated by the European Commission and NATO. There are no more secrets here. The decision for a war economy has been an important step on the road to the apocalypse that Europe is moving on.

In order to better understand what is at stake, we will only briefly recall the needs for the good functioning of a war economy. It will then be easy to see that the USA, on the one hand through NATO, which it leads unchallenged, and also through its financial cartels, such as Black Rock, hold all the important strings in their hands. The war economy is understood to be an economic order, in which a strongly regulating interventionism and a central and planned economy control by the state and its organs are made possible. Civil liberties are being restricted. This is done under the pretext of

---

had the word "war fitness" suggested to him for this. The German President of the European Commission has proposed the appointment of a Commissioner for "Defense".

meeting the requirements of a threat of war. The primary goal of this type of mobilization is to give priority to the provision of goods for war, i.e. weapons, ammunition and military equipment, but also food, primarily to cover the needs of the army. As we can currently observe, it is precisely this policy of a war economy that Ukraine has been consistently following since 2014: everything serves the war. Its own population emigrates in order to be endured and supported by other European countries. The resulting war economy and the resulting arms production are heavily dependent on war financing from Western countries. This economy is not sustainable in itself, but is a tributary of war to be led. It is also increasingly restricting the supply of its own population and the civilian economy. The war economy and the needs of the civilian economy compete for scarce goods. The centralist and authoritarian state decides on the allocation of resources and the regulation of consumption through a bureaucratic distribution system, the efficiency of which ultimately determines the material framework conditions of warfare in the modern age.

Chapter 3

Political Will and Strategic Thinking

This world means something to the capable and is not mute to the brave. Why does he need to roam eternity! Let him grasp what is firm reality.

Goethe, Faust.
The Tragedy, Second Part, 1832. Act 5

In his important historical work on the "Decline of the West, A Morphology of World History", Oswald Spengler presented[35] a comparative analysis and philosophy for the understanding of the classical Greek man and spirit (the Apollonian type) compared with the modern, scientific-technically educated man and spirit (the Faustian type). As an attentive observer of world political events,

---

[35] Spengler says he found the idea for this book in 1913. The first volume was published in 1918, the second volume was published in 1922.

one may feel reminded of these thoughts in the current situation.

To be honest, one cannot help but marvel at the American political will, i.e. the "Faustian will", to assert its interests. It almost arouses a feeling of admiration to see the courage and determination with which the USA has driven the Europeans into the current global conflicts and led them into the new open war against Russia.

Even if this callousness may have grown partly out of a courage of desperation, we honestly cannot avoid admitting that such vehement determination, which is the prerequisite for great wars and major crimes alike[36], has been completely lost in the European countries and their leaders and must often be considered downright unthinkable.

European political leaders are much more likely to radiate a melancholic nostalgia, as we know it from the "Knight of the Rueful

---

[36] In the chapter "Law of Aggression" in his book "The Laws of Human Nature" (2021), Robert Greene cites very convincing examples. This is perhaps even more true of his book "The Laws of Power" (1998).

Countenance".[37] Big words and impressive gestures are at best dared in the American slipstream. Independent, sovereign action can no longer be expected. Europe has dwarfed itself politically in her personalities and follows the example of the small Baltic EU members, who borrow their importance solely from its bigger brother on the other side of the Atlantic and its older siblings from "Brussels".

To be honest, we must also acknowledge that, on the face of it and according to the impression given by the leaders at the global political level, it is the Russian and Chinese role players who are most likely to exude sovereignty on the big stage of world politics that can compete with the United States.

This appearance and our perceptual observation are supported by the fact that, apart from the three large states mentioned above, no nation or confederation of states can define similarly clear geopolitical goals and would also be able to deploy the courage

---

[37] Don Quixote, the "hero" from Miguel de Cervantes' novel, gave himself this nickname on the advice of his squire.

to enforce them in an independent and sovereign way.

Since the admission of the Eastern European countries to the EU and NATO, after 1990, and the accession of France to NATO in 2009, Europe and the EU have finally lined up in order behind the American hegemon.

Apart from the USA, it is only China that, with its *Road and Belt Initiative (RBI)*, the founding of the *Shanghai Cooperation Organization (SCO)*, and the associated large Interbank Consortium, has set the clear geopolitical goal of building an alternative to the Bretton Woods Institutions and the Western world of values. This is China's offer to the Global South and to all the states and nations of the world in search of their independent development.

Under Putin's leadership, Russia has managed to pull the ripcord in time and prevent the sell-off of its natural resources under stress and in difficult times, with great courage and considerable effort. Russia was woken up, due to the war with Ukraine, and is now forced to increasingly build and shape its own political profile at the global level against the combined power of the entire West. The military potential and efficient war technology, in combination with its wealth of natural resources, are the important factors in Russia's ambition to make the Eurasian north and the Central Asian heartlands spheres in which it is recognized for its leading role.

Chapter 4

Overview of the EU's foreign policy role

Within the framework of this study, we cannot attempt to reconstruct the historical evolution of the European Union, or to offer an overall overview of the institutions and status of the European Union. Nevertheless, we want to create a picture in order to put the theses and considerations that we will present here below in a meaningful framework. In doing so, we will be guided by our personal experience that we have been able to gain in professional practice as organizational consultant with various European institutions since 1995, especially in our work with and for the European Commission.

The first point that we would like to emphasize is that the European Union is not a democratic project[38]. It has clearly been

---

[38] In the political discussions on the EU and the European Commission, the "democratic deficit" is repeatedly pointed out, rightly in our view. For an overview:

pushed forward by European political leaders and elites as a joint European initiative. The European Economic Community (EEC) was founded in 1957 with the "Treaties of Rome". The primary goal at that time was to reassure each other that the future in Europe should be shaped without further wars. The subject of these EEC treaties was limited to certain sub-areas and took into account the early realization that a political or even military union could not be achieved immediately. Priority was therefore given to the economy and peace building. This had already been decided earlier by representatives of European elites at the Bilderberg conferences[39] on the preparation of the

---

https://de.wikipedia.org/wiki/Demokratiedefizit_der_E urop%C3%A4ischen_Union#:~:text=Das%20Demokra tiedefizit%20oder%20Europ%C3%A4ischen%20Union, Wirken%20nicht%20ausreichend%20demokratisch%2 olegitimiert.

[39] The Bilderberg Conferences are informal meetings of influential people from Europe from business, politics, the media, academia, the high nobility and secret services, where thoughts on current political, economic and social issues are exchanged and agreements are made. The Bilderberg Group is not a formal organization. The first Bilderberg Conference was held

European community. It is also important to note that Great Britain is not one of the founding members. The United Kingdom, together with Denmark and Ireland, did not join the European Communities until January 1973.

So when we point out this elitist character of the EU, it seems very important to us to emphasize that the EU's most successful and popular program is probably the "Europe of the Regions". This program emerged after 1980 as a political concept intended to promote geographical and historical regions within Europe independently of the direct influence of the EU member states and to support them in their regional independence. It is a kind of integration model in which individual geographical and historical regions in Europe are to be given more sovereignty and strengthened in accordance with the principle of subsidiarity. In this federal system approach, citizens are to be more involved in decision-making. The "Europe of the Regions" program promotes cooperation through joint projects and initiatives that are

in 1954 at the invitation of Prince Bernhard of the Netherlands at his Hotel Bilderberg.

implemented across countries. They can affect economic, cultural or ecological regions as well as promote joint projects. We mention this program because it shows that cooperation between the people in the regions, historical settlement areas and cities concerned in Europe can effectively bring fruitful results and experiences. From this perspective, the evils and problems of the European Union seem to stem more from the political elites in the member states. The Treaty of Maastricht, which came into force in 1993, i.e. under Jacques Delors as head of the European Commission, established the Committee of the Regions as an advisory body of the European Union.

Overall, it must be understood and also positively emphasized that the European Union was created and constantly developed in a constructive process between the member states. So there was no secret plan, or blueprint. Thus, in 1993, the EEC was renamed the European Union by the Treaty of Maastricht. New institutions have also been created again and again, such as the European Court of Justice, to take on common tasks. In 2009, the Treaty of Lisbon established a common set of rules for the functioning and management of the European Union. However, this Treaty of Lisbon, which was originally presented with the ambition of a European Constitution, was not adopted by all parliaments. Nevertheless, it has retained its validity. This, too, is a project of the elites, with deliberate exclusion and without the direct participation of the European population.

An important area that we would like to address briefly here concerns European foreign policy. Even if the creation of the EEC were to have primal significance for Europe's internal affairs, i.e., the economic and political relations of the European Member States, it must not be overlooked that the founding of the EEC and the European Union was also to have a foreign policy significance from the outset. This is already evident in the quite contrasting discussions of the groups that formed early on around the two "founding fathers", Jean Monnet and Robert Schumann. While Jean Monnet had envisaged a European federal state based on the model of the USA from the beginning, Schumann clearly favored a confederation of states in the spirit of Charles de Gaulle's policy, i.e. the so-called "Europe of the Fatherlands". This area of tension basically continues to this day, although it must be said that, at the latest since the reign of German Chancellor Angela Merkel, from 2005 to 2021, the creation of the European federal state based on the model of the USA has progressively taken shape. This irreversibility of the European integration process from the perspective of a European federal state is very convincingly demonstrated in the studies and books of Charles B. Blankart. In 2007, Blankart published his knowledgeable and profound study on *Federalism in Germany and Europe* in the series "New Studies on Political Economy", published by the Nomos Verlag. With regard to the "financial constitution", Blankart shows (on p. 14) how the "paradigm shift in Europe, especially in Germany, against federalism after the First World War" prevailed. From this time on, it had become clear that federalism in its initial form would no longer have a future within the European Union.[40] Today, the unitary central state has

---

[40] The standard work by Charles B. Blankart: "Public Finance in Democracy: An Introduction to Public

already become reality. This development has definitely taken root under Commission President Ursula von der Leyen, first under the pretext of the measures taken during the so-called Corona pandemic and finally in the period after 2022, during the war in Ukraine.

In this context, it is also important to understand that the complex institutional structure of the European Union that has emerged, has largely been created on the model of the French bureaucracy. The main administrative and bureaucratic structures of the EU were put in place during the reign of French President Mitterrand and under the leadership of European Commissioner Jacques Delors. This is certainly one of the reasons why the entire structure of the EU has been strongly modelled on the French centralist presidential system. This centralized structure has subsequently also led to the European Commission (EC), as the central institution, acquiring more and more new powers. This process of "delegation of powers" to the European Commission has been promoted, at least indirectly and steadily, by European governments, because

Finance", Hardcover, 2017.

it has repeatedly enabled European heads of government to make decisions in "Brussels" that would have been difficult to defend at home before their own parliaments. If such "proposals" come from "Brussels", then they are usually just nodded off by the parliaments at home. One thinks of the "euro rescue". It is still true today that the effects of the EU and its institutions, as well as their political and social consequences, are not understood in their real scope by the people or by most politicians in the member states. This understanding exists, if at all, for the most part in the European Parliament, because the parliamentarians there are closer to the actual events and to the proceedings and decision-making processes in "Brussels". However, the European Parliament has still remained largely powerless in the face of the European Commission (EC) and the governments of the Member States. Nor is it a parliament that would adequately represent the European population, as the number of members does not correspond to the respective populations of the member states. Although it also has a so-called "direct democratic legitimacy", it has hardly any decision-making powers, and in particular, it has no budget responsibility.

An important event in the short history of the EU can shed some more light on this institutional scenario and institutional network of the EU, which is often accused of a "democratic deficit". The event we are referring to took place during the term of office of Commission President Jacques Santer, who was in office from 1995 to 1999 and immediately followed the third Commission of Jacques Delors. At that time, the European Court of Auditors received information from the press, which it diligently investigated. Irregularities were uncovered committed by French Commissioner Edith Cresson, a former French prime minister under Mitterrand, which were stigmatized as corruption. Edith Cresson was responsible for the important Commissariat for Science, Research and Development. Due to the intervention of the European Court of Auditors, the entire Commission under Santer had to resign after the European Parliament threatened a motion of censure. It is important for us to note here that the European Court of Auditors has largely lost its influence since this incident. Despite numerous serious irregularities, including in budget management and administration, there have never been consistent results of the work of the European Court of Auditors since 1999. Its reports are practically never discussed or presented to the public in the European public or by the parliaments of the member states. This example shows how important processes of political governance are increasingly faded out of the light of the democratic public. We are not aware of a single one of the many cases reported by the European Court of Auditors since 1999 that would have been taken up by the European public or parliaments in order to investigate them more closely and perhaps even draw conclusions from them. If anything, so-called "democratic deficits" are pointed out by the EC in member states such as Hungary, Poland or Slovakia to justify questionable disciplinary measures against "dissenters from the majority opinion". Progressively and without democratic control by the people, the European central state has submitted to a tendency towards an authoritarian, unitary and coercive state, as it became known in antiquity with the late Roman Empire[41].

A very important step in the formation of institutions within the EU was initiated in 1993 with the creation of a Common Foreign and Security Policy (CFSP) of the European Union. The main objectives of this CFSP are officially "to preserve peace, strengthen international security, promote international cooperation and develop and consolidate democracy, the rule of law and respect for human rights and fundamental freedoms[42]". It was not until 1999 that the European Council introduced[43] the post of High Representative for the CFSP, i.e. a kind of

---

[41] These historical developments of the Roman Empire towards an authoritarian, unitary and coercive state is superbly described by Theodor Mommsen in The History of Rome, and in particular by Edward Gibbon in The History and Decline of the Roman Empire.
[42]

https://www.europarl.europa.eu/factsheets/de/sheet/1 58/eu-au%C3%9Fenpolitik-ziele-mechanismen-und-ergebnisse

[43] The European Council is the body of the heads of state or government of the European Union. At least twice every six months, the Council meets for a meeting, also known as an EU summit.

European Foreign Commissioner. With a further decision of the European Council in 2001, the Political and Security Committee (PSC) was created with the intention of assuming political control and strategic orientation for the management of international crises.

We would like to make a few important comments on this topic of Common Foreign and Security Policy that are important for understanding the EU's self-image and must be taken into account when reading the following chapters in this book. We want to refer to some very important developments that are practically unknown to the European public. These developments have taken place in recent decades and should be well understood to better appreciate the role of the EU as an actor on the international stage and in the context of global developments.

Starting from its original focus on European domestic policy, i.e. the focus on economic and political relations between the member states of the EEC, a European Union has progressively emerged that increasingly intended to play a role on the stage of international politics and within the international political and economic decision-making processes.

This new role was consciously and strategically developed by Mitterrand and Delors, who had a strong influence on the EU during their periods of government and activity, mainly from 1985 to 1994. France wanted to pursue policies to promote the importance and influence of France as the "Grande Nation" and, if possible, to strengthen its role, i.e. to play off the influence of the "Grande Nation" through the EU with a potentiated power, so to speak. Historically and at the institutional level, European foreign policy arose from the centralization of the European development policy[44], which had put the EU into a position

---

[44] The development policy institutions of the member states were not abolished after 1993. But the vast majority of development funding has been handed over to the EU for use in accordance with EU rules. Originally, most of the funds went to the ACP (African-Caribbean-Pacific) countries. After 1990, extensive programs for the economic development of the countries of Central and Eastern Europe were launched and financed by the EBRD – European Bank for Reconstruction and Development, under its French bank president, a personal friend of Mitterrand.

to act confidently and effectively as a global actor and with relatively generous resources at a very early stage.

Promoted mainly by France, and in the spirit of the European transfer of financial and economic power from the "wealthier" to the less prosperous states, the European Investment Bank (EIB) was founded as early as 1958 with the task of promoting European economic policy by lending with its own capital resources "in order to contribute to a balanced and smooth development of the internal market in the interest of the Union"[45]. After 1990, i.e. after the dissolution of the Soviet Union, the EBRD – European Bank for Reconstruction and Development[46] – was another important instrument created primarily to finance the construction of

---

[45] We will see later that the requirements of managing the Marshall Fund—this first centralized European instrument has been created. Ref. to our footnotes on the Marshall-fund and the studies and books by Hans-Werner Sinn and Abelshauser.

[46] The first president of the EBRD was Jacques Attali, a long-time advisor to Mitterand. For a long time, Attali was considered one of the most influential personalities, globally. He has also published many books on various topics.

infrastructure in the new and future member states of the EU in Central, Eastern and Southeastern Europe.

At this point, we would like to note that the creation and development of the EU has been observed internationally with great interest and often even with applause and admiration. A unique and exemplary process seemed to have been set in motion to bring states together peacefully and in mutual interest. In this way, the EU has become a model for many international and regional alliances and associations of states in Asia, Africa and Latin America. So it is no wonder that at this time there has been talk of a multipolar world, with the EU as an important and exemplary new "non-aligned" actor. The most important principle promoted by the EU's foreign and development policy, from 1960 to about 2000, has been "partnership" between equal and sovereign partners. The EU has offered her partnership to countries and nations around the world with the purpose of working together to create and shape a better, more peaceful, and more prosperous world.

However, after the event of 9/11 in 2001, i.e. the destruction of the Twin Towers of the

World Trade Center, this orientation of European foreign policy was to change fundamentally. As late as 2003, there was still considerable resistance from Europe to the imperialist policy of the USA[47], which was forcefully demonstrated by the wars in Iraq and Afghanistan. However, this resistance did not last long, and the EU was increasingly drawn into the orbit of US foreign policy interests. The principle of partnership ultimately gave rise to "association agreements" and other legal structures, with which the previous EU partners were forced to exercise political obedience and adopt a neoliberal economic policy course. Only under these conditions did the EU allocate financial resources to the partner countries. Freedom of choice was increasingly restricted for the partner countries.

An authoritarian style then increasingly prevailed within the European Commission. Opposition to the policy of "association agreements" in line with the economic and political interests of the EU, and in harmony with the USA, was not tolerated anymore. In

---

[47] We refer here to the corresponding chapters in the book "Colossus" by Niall Ferguson.

the meantime, in 2009, France had also joined NATO. Increasingly, the economic and political interests of the EU have been linked to the military interests of NATO. As we will show in the relevant chapters here in our study, Europe has completely lost its sovereignty over a creeping political process of about a hundred years. This is arguably one of the biggest event for Europe since the French Revolution. At that time, the hope for freedom-equality-fraternity arose in Europe. After 2001 times have changed, and we in Europe have once again entered the dark age of ideological polarization and armed conflicts, civil wars and wars, which we had believed to be over after 1945 and with the creation of the European Union as a 'peace project'. It seems fateful for Europe, as if the evil demon of discord, strife and wars does not want to let us escape from its claws.

Chapter 5

Europe the "common home" – Russia the eternal enemy

We drafted this chapter with the intention to also open up a positive perspective on Europe and the EU, with a kind of vision that is unfortunately not shared by the United States, because it obviously contradicts its interests in global hegemony and dominance over Europe. The first Secretary General of NATO, Lord Hastings Lionel Ismay, already made the remark that Russia should be kept out, the Americans should be in, and the Germans should be kept down[48]. It should be noted that this was not only about NATO, but also about Europe as a geopolitical entity. In an interview, Jacques Baud, a graduate in

---

[48] Quoted from https://www. NATO.int/cps/en/NATOhq/declassified_137930.htm. - Lord Hastings Lionel Ismay was NATO's first Secretary General, a position he was initially reluctant to accept. By the end of his tenure, however, Ismay had become the biggest advocate of the organization he had famously said earlier on in his political career: "It was created to keep the Soviet Union out, the Americans in, and the Germans down."

international security at the Graduate Institute of International Relations in Geneva, former colonel in the Swiss Army, and employee of the Swiss Strategic Intelligence Service, expresses himself on this subject in a clear way as follows: "The policy of the United States has always been to prevent Germany and Russia from working more closely together."[49] This point of view is common knowledge in US-European studies and is presented in many relevant books.[50]

The positive perspective and vision that we want to mention here refer to the concept of the so-called Greater Europe, which includes the rapprochement and gradual integration of Russia and European countries. As is well known, French President Charles de Gaulle

---

[49] Interview recorded on 05.04.22, by Thomas Kaiser for Current Affairs in Focus. Quoted in Presenza – International Press Agency: https://www.pressenza.com/2022/04.

[50] Refer to Eckart Conze; Die gaullistische Herausforderung. Die deutsch-französischen Beziehungen in der amerikanischen Europapolitik 1958–1963, München 1995; oder auch vom selben Autor: Die große Illusion. Versailles 1919 und die Neuordnung der Welt, 2018.

famously spoke out in 1959 in[51] favor of an alliance from the Atlantic to the Urals, which "will decide the fate of the world". This idea was also taken up again in 1985 by Mikhail Gorbachev, then General Secretary of the Central Committee of the Communist Party of the Soviet Union (CPSU).[52] He turned this into a call to see Europe as the "common home".[53] Remarkably, this idea was taken up and developed after 1990 by the governments of Russia, jointly with the European Union and its main member states. The Partnership and Cooperation Agreement

---

[51] Le voyage présidentiel en Alsace, 1959.

[52] The visit of the General Secretary of the CPSU Central Committee, Mikhail Gorbachev, to France in 1985.

[53] Anyone who wants to devalue such an initiat ve for cooperation with the use of the term "Eurasianism" only makes it clear that he is concerned with defamation, but not with finding modalities for peaceful cooperation.

In the title of the essay "Rule from Lisbon to Vladivostok", by Robert Hahn, to which we refer here, "rule" is also in the foreground. There is no talk of cooperation here. An "obscure ideology" is suspected behind this proposal of European cooperation, which has mutated into a fascist battle cry for "Russian exiled intellectuals". Yes, in this way, you can refuse dialogue.

between the EU and Russia was signed as early as 1994.[54] The focus here was still clearly on economic cooperation and the creation of the necessary conditions for the future establishment of a free trade area.

We should point out here that such partnership agreements have been concluded by the EU with many states on all continents. So this is in no way about a special privilege for Russia.[55] In order to make the partnership

---

[54] Agreement on partnership and cooperation establishing a partnership between the European Communities and their Member States, of one part, and the Russian Federation, of the other part, 1994.

[55] For the unbiased reader, we should also note that the EU also offers so-called association agreements. These are to be classified higher than partnership agreements.

These association agreements are international treaties that the European Union concludes with third countries in order to establish special relations with each other. The priorities of stabilization and association agreements between the EU and third countries differ. Depending on the structure, the associated partner is granted different mutual rights and obligations. These association agreements between the EU and third countries serve to bring the EU closer together on the way to a possible later accession to the EU, such as the agreements with

agreement with Russia more concrete, a group was convened in 2001 with the support of the President of the European Commission, Romano Prodi, to develop a project for a common European economic area.[56] In the same year, Russian President Vladimir Putin explained the importance of close trade and economic relations between Russia and the EU in a landmark speech in Germany to the Bundestag.[57] This was followed by the adoption of the *roadmap* for

---

Turkey and the Western Balkan states. However, association agreements have also been concluded with countries such as Tunisia, Israel, Morocco, Jordan, Egypt and Algeria. Such agreements with these countries primarily serve trade policy, but also migration and security policy.

[56] Joint Statement on the Energy Dialogue by President of the Russian Federation Vladimir Putin, President of the European Council Guy Verhofstadt, with the assistance of the Secretary General of the Council of the EU/High Representative for the Common Foreign and Security Policy Javier Solana, and President of the European Commission Romano Prodi, 2001.

[57] From the protocol of Vladimir Putin's speech in the German Bundestag, 2001.

the common economic area in 2005.[58] In 2010, Putin proposed *the creation of a free trade zone from Lisbon to Vladivostok* in an article in the Süddeutsche Zeitung.[59] This idea was increasingly understood as part of Russia's foreign policy.[60] Finally, the harmonization and development of European and Eurasian integration were formulated as strategic tasks in relation to the EU. The creation of a common economic and humanitarian space from the Atlantic to the Pacific has thus been declared an important goal of Russian foreign policy.[61]

In contrast, Russia was increasingly critical of its political relations with the United States. In his speech at the 2007 Munich Conference on Security Policy, Putin criticized the monopolistic dominance of the United States in global relations, claiming that the United States was displaying an "almost unrestrained

---

[58] EU and Russia: A roadmap for the Common Economic Space (CES), 2005.

[59] Putin, 2010.

[60] Foreign Policy Concept of the Russian Federation, 2013.

[61] Foreign Policy Concept of the Russian Federation, 2016.

use of hyper-force in international relations."
He went on to say that the result is that "no
one feels safe! ... Of course, such a policy
promotes an arms race."[62] In an interview in
January 2007, Putin declared that Russia was
in favor of a democratic, multipolar world and
the strengthening of the international legal
system.[63] In his speech in 2008, at the
celebration of "Victory Day" against Nazi
Germany, Putin warned with regret that "the
threats are not diminishing, but merely
changing and appearing in a new guise. These
new threats follow the same contempt for
human life and the same efforts to establish
exclusive domination over the whole
world."[64] At the 33rd G8 summit in June 2007,
Putin said to the USA: "We do not want
confrontation; rather, we want to offer
ourselves for dialogue. However, we demand
that this dialogue recognize the equality of
the interests of both sides." However, Russia

---

[62] You can find it in the reports on the 43rd Security
Conference in Munich.

[63] Indian Television Channel Doordarshan and Press
Trust of India News Agency, 18 January 2007.

[64] Transcript of the speech in the Kremlin archives,
March 5, 2008.

saw its security interests increasingly called into question. NATO expanded eastward in further steps by accepting the former countries of the Eastern Bloc as members. Missiles were stationed in the countries of Eastern Europe, and NATO was getting closer and closer to Russia's borders in a threatening way.

Parallel to these increasingly tense developments on the political side, the rapprochement on the economic side was nevertheless pushed forward.[65] There were still forces within the EU that did not want to give up the economic advantages of relations with Russia. In February 2017, the German *economic research institute IFO* published an article in which it considered the free trade zone from Lisbon to Vladivostok not only feasible, but also beneficial for both sides.[66] In June 2019, an important delegation of representatives of the EU and the Eurasian Economic Commission met for a meeting. The aim of the meeting was to promote

---

[65] In Germany, this policy of economic relations with Russia under the government of Willy Brandt was described by the slogan "Change through Trade".

[66] Felbermayr, G., & Gröschl, J., 2017.

dialogue on the technical aspects of trade policy, technical regulation, customs legislation, and digitalization, as well as the exchange of information on the regulatory framework of mutual interest.[67] In the summer of 2019, after a meeting with Russian President Putin, French President Emmanuel Macron published a post via social media in which he pretended that he "considers Russia to be a deeply European country and believes in a Europe that stretches from Lisbon to Vladivostok".[68]

It will not have escaped our notice that these encouraging diplomatic initiatives, notes and remarks by the EU and its member states took place at a time when the implementation of the Minsk agreements of 2015 was actively obstructed by the same states. During these years, the Ukrainian government bombed and maltreated the two Russian-speaking regions of Luhansk and Donetsk on a daily basis, with an estimated 14,000 people falling victim to these military

---

[67] Eurasian Economic Commission and European Commission are building technical dialogue, 2019.
[68] Blogging on Facebook in Russian, Macron notes progress in ties with Moscow, 2019.

attacks, which were carried out by its own Ukrainian government and covered by the European states and the USA. So it is only understandable that the Russian government must have asked itself more and more what exactly had to be done to end this situation.

During these talks and negotiations on cooperation between the EU and Russia, the lack of common values was repeatedly and critically emphasized in the statements of Western political leaders. At the same time, it was repeatedly emphasized that Russia's relations with the western part of Europe should "normalize" and that the Russian leadership must recognize that Russia is ultimately a European and not a Eurasian state.[69] For Russia, acceding to this demand of the Western states would have meant giving up an important part of its identity and history. This identity of Russia includes historical relations with the Central Asian peoples, as well as the peculiarity of its geographical location as the central northern part of the Euro-Asian continent. This demand from Western Europe was and is

---

[69] Bratersky, 2017.

therefore ultimately unrealistic and ne ther historically nor geographically justified.[70]

---

[70] One of many sources: The Cambridge History of Russia, edited by Dominic Lieven, 2005. An overview with references to the history of Russia can be found on Wikipedia.

Chapter 6

The New World Order after the Treaty of Versailles

"The question is, how can we get away from the rules, within which we... since the Treaty of Versailles, are proceeding politically. The challenge is to change the rules..."

"Ecology of the Mind,
Part VI, Crises in the Ecology of the Mind",
1966 lecture "From Versailles to Cybernetics",
Gregory Bateson

FOREWORD

Only a few people in 1919 could have imagined how important the political decisions after the First World War would be for the future coexistence on our planet. After the end of the British Empire, the European monarchies and the classical bourgeoisie, the age of democracies, globalization and US hegemony was heralded.

Even if the lives of people, on a large as well as on a small scale, do not follow a plan, it is nevertheless astonishing to see how a red thread runs through the history of mankind over the last hundred years.

LIFE IN A CRISIS MODE - SYMPTOMS OF GLOBAL POLITICAL STRUCTURES

A hundred years ago, American President Woodrow Wilson established a foreign policy doctrine that was, in his understanding, intended to avoid future global conflicts and secure US interests through the worldwide spread of a market economy and democracy and, in cases of emergency, through military interventions in trouble spots.[71] The term Wilsonianism was coined when Wilson

---

[71] There is a vast amount of literature on the subject of the Treaty of Versailles, the negotiations, and its significance. For a quick access and to clarify the significance for American hegemonic politics, we recommend: "Colossus: The Rise and Fall of the American Empire", 2004, by Niall Ferguson. A summary worth reading with bibliography can be found on Wikipedia:
https://de.wikipedia.org/wiki/Friedensvertrag_von_Ver sailles

presented his 14-point program "for eternal peace" in Europe in 1918, even before the negotiations on the Treaty of Versailles had been launched at the end of the First World War[72]. Wilsonianism had thus set itself the goal of showing the world the way out of a "global" crisis[73]. Wilson is considered in the

---

[72] With the arguments summarized in the 14-point program of the then President Wilson of 1918, he had already justified the entry of the USA into the First World War before the US Congress and the American public. Also compare the anthology by Jens Heisterkamp (ed.), Die Jahrhundertillusion. Wi son's Right of Self-Determination of Peoples, Steiner's Critique and the Question of the National Minorities of Today, Frankfurt/Main, 2002. This anthology was very competently reviewed in the journal Perseus, der Europäer, Vol. 6 No. 8, June 2002, by Andreas Bracher, under the title "Völkische Selbstbestimmung und Dreigliederung".

[73] Compare, among others, the British economist John Maynard Keynes, who attended the negotiations on behalf of the British government at the time and already clearly named the nonsense of Clemenceau's French negotiating position at the time. An important source is also the essay "From Versailles to Cybernetics" by Gregory Bateson, published in: Ecology of the Mind, Suhrkamp Wissenschaft 571, Frankfurt 1985, which unfortunately was never published, but provides important insights into this

USA as a president who personally represented high and noble standards and also initiated some meaningful initiatives.[74] However, two points were decisive in this historically important moment: on the one hand, the USA claimed the right for themselves, it even considered it its duty to ensure peace in the future mainly in Europa, but finally at a global stage, if necessary by force of arms. The second important point concerns the fact that he allowed the revanchist claims of France and Britain against Germany to pass without objection in the Treaty of Versailles. As a result, Europe

---

process of the Versailles negotiations. Important points for us here: (a) The Treaty of Versailles, also sometimes called the Dictate of Versailles, was the starting point for the Second World War, which led Europe, including the Soviet Union, under the Nazis and fascists led by Hitler into another catastrophe. Wilsonianism, which was launched at the same time, was the beginning of Pax Americana, i.e. the claim of the Americans to bring "peace and democracy" to the world under their leadership.

[74] See Lesson 62: World War I – The Road to Intervention" and Lesson 63: "World War I – Versailles and Wilson's Gambit" from the book "The History of the United States, 2nd Edition, 2003, by C. Guelzo, Gary Gallagher, and Patrick N. Allitt.

finally moved in the direction of the catastrophe of the Second World War that was already lurking. Instead of looking for a constructive way out of the dilemma, Europe had finally continued on the path that would lead to the destruction of its own historical significance in the future. The result was that USA had become the big winner of the First World War.[75]

No one has analyzed more prophetically than John Maynard Keynes, why the Treaty of Versailles had to trigger a new war and political conflicts that are still smoldering today.[76] Keynes' polemical essay contains a clear reference to the unregained level of Europe's wealth before 1914 and the bleak outlook on the less than hopeful post-war period. No one else has described so vividly and with analytical mockery, how peace was gambled away in 1919 and incalculable damage was inflicted on Europe. In doing so,

---

[75] We should not mention here that the United States insisted on repaying the loans it had lent to France and Great Britain during the war years, even before it joined the war.

[76] War and Peace. The Economic Consequences of the Treaty of Versailles, 1920, John Maynard Keynes.

he offers at the same time important insights into the psychology and behavior, as well as the particular interests of Woodrow Wilson, Lloyd George and Georges Clemenceau, the negotiators on the American, British and French sides[77]. Thus, shortly after the "primordial catastrophe"[78] and the brief regain of a spirit of optimism in the "wild" 20s, Europe soon switched back into crisis mode, from which we have not been able to get out to this day, even though we have created great material wealth in the meantime through strong economic growth after 1949. Apart from brief breathers in the 1920s and from 1950 to 1970, which gave cause for optimism, the splendor of the European world powers was rapidly fading, and the age

---

[77] Keynes refrained from commenting on David Lloyd George, the British negotiator. Obviously, he didn't want to make enemies at home.

[78] Historians refer to the First World War as a "primordial catastrophe". This designation goes back to the American historian and diplomat George F. Kennan, who characterized the war in 1979 as "the great seminal catastrophe of this century". A differentiated interpretation will appreciate the war as a cipher for the end of the bourgeoisie and for the "crisis of classical modernity".

of European global dominance was inexorably approaching its historic end.

We still live and develop today in this apparent mode of increasing crisis in Europe. So we should not be surprised if our media and political leaders make us believe that we in Europe have been threatened by a whole series of crises since 2007. This is how we read on Wikipedia about the crises that were emerging and ongoing at this time: *The world economic crisis from 2007 onwards was triggered by the bursting of a real estate bubble (in the USA; our note), with the accompanying financial crisis and banking crisis, which was later followed by sovereign debt crises, and sometimes state crises, as in Greece.*

A number of years have passed since 2007. At that time, as we have seen, the world was in the midst of a major economic crisis, accompanied by other important crises. The real estate price bubble or sub-prime bubble in the USA had burst. We were all affected by the so-called Lehman banking crisis.

Obviously, we should be afraid for our money, for our livelihoods and for our way of life. Not yet for our lives. That's what we were told, and we reacted accordingly and were ready, if not to accept everything, then at least ready to bear burdens "without alternative".

Since then, we have been living in crisis mode, which has intensified in the past decade. This mood is led by the media, by politicians and scientists of all stripes, who try to offer us explanations for everything that has just happened and is happening again and again. They all offered their stories and steered the world with this consistency of public mood. In the European Union (EU), the so-called sovereign debt crisis was soon added to this scenario. The euro crisis was then still an additional gift to politicians. In this way, they were able to make it clear to all of us: we could only do as well as before, if we made more effort and were willing to make more sacrifices. We were told to listen to our politicians and the responsible power elites — they certainly would know what to do and what is best for all of us[79].

---

[79] In the media, even at the highest level, we are informed that the "state quota" has been rising steadily since then. This points to increasing centralization and the strengthening of the unitary state.

Oh yes, and elsewhere "there were other and more crisis"; new crises arose again and again. In Syria, Iraq and Afghanistan, war has been waged on a large scale. The Arab Spring broke out in the Northern African states in 2011, with massive unrest and civil war-like conditions in some cases. It didn't take long before Yemen was also heavily bombed. Saudi Arabia obviously had a great interest in finally being able to use its air force with the opportunity to deploy the expensive American bombers, while the USA also had a great interest in doing so, because they had to provide training, for adequate payment, of course, and supply the ammunition, as well as secure supplies for destroyed or shot down aircraft. We all became witness of an old philosophy saying that every crisis provides opportunities to make comfortable profits.

Clearly, there has been a lot going on in the world over the past years and decades.

We should not forget the various color revolutions, or should we say attempted *coups d'etat*, some non-violent protests, as in the case of Georgia, some not successful, as in the case Belarus and Kyrgyzstan, others leading to the outbreak of a war with the deployment of NATO aircraft and nuclear ammunition, as it has been the case in former Yugoslavia. From today's perspective, it is very important to mention the "spring revolution" of 2014 on the Maidan in Kyiv, with the subsequent coup in Ukraine and the Crimean crisis. In addition, there is the constant and increasingly felt threat, albeit mostly promoted by our media, from China, whose economy threatens to buy up all of us here in Europe, and which, as a state in Asia, threatens and wants to colonize not only a few atolls, but the entire Pacific world and is now in a "trade war" with the whole world[80]. We take all this from our media every day, and are called upon by modern methods of "framing" to believe our "responsible" elites

---

[80] This geopolitical situation is also the reason for the "Achberg Peace Initiative", as it was initiated by Herbert Schliffka and associated friends as a consequence of the "Achberg Impulse for Freedom, Direct Democracy and Global Solidarity in Economic Life" (https://kulturzentrum-achberg.de/). Schliffka provides the framework for this very well in the essay "Geopolitical Strategies: Dangers for a Self-Determined Europe? – Achberger Beiträge für ein "gemeinsame Haus Europa" im 21.

and their noble representatives and to follow them faithfully.

And let us also remember the other European crises that we were able to "experience" during this time. We are constantly threatened by immigrants, some have been invited and then uninvited again. Europe is splitting, Great Britain has split off from the EU in a Brexit, and the Eastern European member states of the EU allow themselves to express their own positions in different areas and do not want to continue being patronized by the Western European member states, such as France and Germany.

Reality is complex, and it is not always easy to understand the processes and to make them understandable[81]. However, that is what we intend to do here in our book, at least to some extent.

---

[81] In his lectures of 1919 on the symptomatology of history, Rudolf Steiner challenges us to see the reality behind the symptoms, the truth behind the events.

THE NEW ORDER OF THE WORLD IS HERALDED BY THE USA IN 1919

When the present series of the so-called crisis started in 2007, it was only one step on the way. The 20th century has been an "age of extremes"[82] and it ended in crises that found their "natural" continuation in the 21st century.

As early as the beginning of the 20th century, more precisely towards the end of the First World War, Europe and the world were to be finally, if not saved, then finally put on the right track, first through the entry of the USA into the war, and then through the implementation of US President Wilson's 14-points program. It was "Wilsonianism" that had been launched by the USA as a by-product of the Treaty of Versailles, together with the initiation of the League of Nations. What France and England would negotiate with the defeated Germany was not so decisive from the point of view of the USA. Much more important was the new doctrine of the American foreign policy, which, in a

[82] The Age of Extremes, World History of the 20th Century, 1995, Eric Hobsbawm.

decisive turn, set itself apart from the previous policy of non-interference in European affairs and separation of global spheres of influence[83]. In the future, the USA would limit itself to the American hemisphere, but bring peace all over the world, if necessary, also by force and through wars. The League of Nations, which the US has never joined, was supposed to provide a diplomatic platform for international dialogue. The major purpose was to facilitate the management of global public opinion and to secure the dominance of the USA in the international arena. This was the core of Wilsonianism, which provided the model for the United Nations (UN) and the Security Council to this day, and justifies every war led by the USA and its allies in NATO, from Vietnam to Afghanistan, then from Iraq to

---

[83] It should not go unmentioned that this policy of hegemony was not initially implemented by the United States, since domestic politics tended to be limited to the American hemisphere. The hegemonic claim of the USA was ultimately a consequence of the Second World War and was only finally initiated by the then President Roosevelt.

Syria, Libya and Yemen, and today in Ukraine[84].

As we know, wars, the most important instrument of foreign policy alongside diplomacy, must also be financed[85]. For this

---

[84] For example, it could be used to justify Turkey's invasion of Syria from 2017 to 2018.

[85] Three important sources should suffice here to underline the pragmatic intelligence of the Americans. The first US Secretary of the Treasury, Alexander Hamilton, understood "financing" as a crucial means of shaping policy and created important instruments for this purpose. Some historians therefore call the USA "Hamilton's Republic".

The Ascent of Money: A Financial History of the World, 2008, Niall Ferguson. In this book, Ferguson shows that the most important political importance of banks, both private and central banks, is the financing of wars.

The Federal Reserve System: its origin and growth; reflections and recollections; 2 volumes, New York, 1930, Paul Moritz Warburg. Paul M. Warburg, a banker from Hamburg, is considered the main initiator of the US central bank FED, which was founded in 1913. In 1921, Paul M. Warburg became the founding chairman of the Council on Foreign Relations (CFR), the most important institution for the coordination of American policy by its elites, with a focus on international relations.

The Creature from Jekyll Island, 1994, George Edward Griffin.

purpose, the USA had created the American central bank, the Federal Reserve Bank (FED) in 1913. As we will see in further detail, this was decisive step towards implementation of the American hegemonic policy, because it provided the financial basis and enabled covering up for the increasing needs for funding of wars, through a steadily increasing amount of loans and debt that have grown to exorbitant dimensions to this day.[86]

When American banks stumbled in 2007, because the repayment of cheap mortgages and loans was no longer guaranteed, the then US President George W. Bush was asked whether he wanted to save Lehmann Bank at the expense of the taxpayers. That was the moment, when this courageous and determined president, following the advice of his high-profile Wall Street-hardened financial and economic advisers, said that he didn't want that. The result was: Lehman

---

[86] A very good overview with impressive graphs of the historical development and current perspective of the debt of the USA can be found in an article by the Kantonalbank Zürich. Sources: Zürcher Kantonalbank, CBO, Census, OMB.
https://www.zkb.ch/de/blog/anlegen/us-staatsverschuldung-rekordkurs.html.

Brothers had to file for bankruptcy. The financial bubble burst. This opened the way for rapid write-downs and a quick and expedient way out of the crisis for the financial cartels and banks of the USA. New opportunities would arise also out of this crisis.

EVERYTHING HAS ITS PRICE, ESPECIALLY FOR GERMANY

The stupid thing for us Europeans was that most of these largely unsecured American mortgages and loans — so-called sub-prime credits — had been passed on from American to European banks, including Deutsche Bank, Commerzbank, and also to some big Irish banks[87]. Therefore, in the end, due to the decisions of the leading European leaders, especially French and German politicians, central bankers and other responsible persons, the European taxpayers had to pay back the bad loans of the American banks. Thus, Europe already contributed to a large

---

[87] Incidentally, this has also contributed to the further decline of Deutsche Bank and Commerzbank, which, by international standards, are now only insignificant.

extent to the financing of the American economy, its armaments industry and the war machine. Cost and risk sharing within NATO has always been an important issue from the point of view of the USA.

At the same time, as a result of the financial crisis in the USA, the euro crisis suddenly arose in Europe, triggered by the so-called sovereign debt crisis.[88] After all, the banks and their owners and investors wanted their money back, if possible with a good return. The norm was the 25 percent return, which Deutsche Bank regularly set as a target at

---

[88] In an article by the State Agency for Civic Education in Baden-Württemberg, it says: "The euro crisis has been a crisis within the European Union that has been going on since 2009. It combines aspects of a sovereign debt crisis, a banking crisis and a financial crisis. In some EU countries, increased borrowing led to high inflation. This could no longer be regulated by a national fiscal policy, so that permanent current account deficits led to high national debt."

It should only be briefly noted here that the debt of the states has continued to grow steadily since that time. No one has seen a "proper" way out for a long time. With seeing eyes, the world, at least the "Western" world, is heading more and more towards the abyss.

that time, but which is often exceeded by the Anglo-Saxon banks and funds to this day[89].

The German government, in close cooperation with France and the European Central Bank (ECB), did what it was asked to do and financed all claims, both those of the banks and those of the EU Member States. The parliament in Germany, as the formal representative of the voters and taxpayers, approved all payments without exception. There was no alternative, at least that's what the then President of the ECB, Jean-Claude Trichet, said, and so the Chancellor and the German government repeated it.

What actually happened in these years of the euro crisis and during the so-called global and also European structural adjustment, should not surprise us anymore. These "structural adjustments" have been led by the FED, the ECB, which may be considered a subsidiary of the FED, which have been assisted by the

---

[89] "The 25 percent is not set in stone, but it is a benchmark that the best in the world have achieved," said top banker Josef Ackermann, head of Deutsche Bank, from 2006 to 2012, about his goal of achieving a return on equity of 25 percent before taxes.

Bretton Woods institutions. Tacitly and without the general public being aware of it, the takeover of the European industries and finance institutions was gaining pace again and has been consistently implemented in just a few years by the Anglo-American capital and their funding institutions, banks and financial cartels. The last remnants of resistance were overcome non-violently. For the Americans it was like a fairy tale, similar to the "fall of the Wall" for the Germans, because everything happened without violence. Europe had capitulated non-violently and given away all their assets.

Everyone was happy. The people in Europe, that it had not gotten worse, and the US investors, because they were able to take over Europe's economy and the management of European capital and the European economy to a majority of extent and on favorable terms without much effort[30]. With

---

[30] The investment funds are now majority owners of entire sectors in the Dax. This means that they not only own majorities in individual companies, but also banks. Rather, they are majority-owned by entire industries, which they can then control more or less at will. It is no longer the individual company or the individual bank that determines its policies, prices and wages. The

the purpose of further smoothing these processes, the EU installed a former Goldman Sachs executive as president of the European Central Bank (ECB). In the U.S., at least since the administration of Bill Clinton, then under Robert Rubin, the Treasury Department has continuously been firmly in the hands of Goldman Sachs, or other leaders of Wall Street and the financial cartels.

In the US, the crisis was therefore only a kind of new start, while in Europe it led to a strong and final shift in the historical claims to power and to the end of financial and economic autonomy. European industry, together with

---

corporate policy and, thus, the socially relevant decisions are made by the investment funds. These are therefore approaching the capacity for economic OVERALL CONTROL. Perhaps they already have this capacity for the most important key industries — in Germany, mechanical engineering and vehicle construction, together with the defense industry, including robotics and other high-tech companies, the chemical industry — and the banks, which have now become "operationally" irrelevant and no longer operate independently. Compare: Has everything been done yet? Focus Magazine, No. 8, 2009, Who Owns Germany?
In 2024, there is not a single company in the DAX in which Black Rock would not have a stake.

banks and financial institutions, was henceforth firmly in the grip of Anglo-American banks, financial institutions and financial cartels. After the crisis of 2007/08, they didn't have to get up and back on their feet, but thanks to their global and huge investment funds, they were immediately and always ready to continue financing the course of the world. After all, business had to go on — because we all wanted to continue to do our, more or less, important business.

The Anglo-American investment funds thus took advantage of this time, when money was scarce in the EU, and companies and banks were often at their limits, especially in Southern Europe. They helped us in Europe by making numerous strategic investments and taking over many "struggling" companies, often directly, but mostly by taking over majorities through their investment funds. In the meantime, the DAX companies listed on the German stock exchange are under the ownership of Anglo-Saxon capital by more than 50 percent[91]. In

[91] Report of the FAZ, "Many American investors, The Dax is firmly in foreign hands", by Daniel Mohr, JANUARY 26, 2017. – These statistics do not include

addition, in the years after 2008, a large number of medium-sized companies in Europe were also bought up by American companies and by Anglo-American capital. This clear trend intensified again to an incredible level after 2022, when the German government opened up their principal industries, such as car and machine production, as well as tool making, to progressive deindustrialization accompanied by further economic and political dependence on the US. In the meantime, the large power grids in Europe are already being taken over by US companies, such as Westinghouse. So one cannot actually speak of energy security anymore. Rather, a new and even more exclusive dependence has emerged, which now includes France and other important countries in Europe, such as Italy, Spain, Poland and the Netherlands.[92]

---

cross-ownership, i.e. if Deutsche Bank owns a share in a company, then this is attributed to Deutsche Bank. Meanwhile, Deutsche Bank is already majority-owned by foreigners.

[92] The Chair of Energy for Society at the de Grenoble Ecole de Management (GEM) of the University of Grenoble is now asking itself "how Europe can prevent its blindness in the field of energy policy (Politiques

The transfer to these global Anglo-American investment funds of the most important real estate assets in Germany and throughout Europe corresponds to another takeover of European assets. What in the past belonged mainly to municipalities, trade union associations or state institutions has now often gone to global investment funds, which adorn themselves with German or European names in order to present themselves as nice German and European companies, demonstrating, how close they are to the citizen. We have just received news reporting how a US hedge fund is buying up a Spanish municipality by taking over its debts. Returns on this investment are not publicly discussed. We do not want to go into detail here about the debts of German and European municipalities, including with foreign investors, which they have taken on to finance their investments and operations[93].

énergétiques : comment éviter une dystopie européenne?) and at the same time warns against selling off to Anglo-American and Chinese investors.

[93] The German Association of Cities commented: "At the end of 2022, the municipalities and associations of municipalities, including their shareholdings, were indebted to the non-public sector with 313.9 billion

The policy of the USA therefore does not serve "to ward off EU competition" on the world markets, i.e. as an industry location policy, but the policy of the USA represents the incorporation of Europe and its states as vassals.[94]

We were all so happy that the German economy was humming again after 2009. We should all be happy about it. Even though a large number of temporary jobs have now been introduced, this has subsequently and increasingly led to precarious living conditions and the threat of poverty in old age. Even the employees of the prisons in Bavaria are now forced to pursue additional gainful employment activities in order to be able to finance their livelihoods[95]. The media report daily on the poor situation of most employees in the "nursing professions". Nevertheless, we should all be happy that there is enough work for everyone, which

---

euros, according to a model calculation by the statistical offices of the federal and state governments. This corresponded to a debt of 4,034 euros per capita.

[94] Refer to cit. Brzezinski.

[95] FAZ, from January 2, 2018, Bavaria, First the prison, then the part-time job.

gives us cause for great happiness every day. In all this, the EU had managed, albeit at an immense economic and political cost, to hold Europe together. Truly, a remarkable result.

EUROPE: BRIDGE BETWEEN EAST AND WEST, OR OUTPOST OF US HEGEMONY

When the EU created the European External Action Service (CFSP) at the beginning of the 21st century, it was supposed to become a "service for peace, security and conflict resolution". How is it then that Europe is increasingly affected by crises and threatened by wars and becomes directly and indirectly involved in them, as in Syria, Libya, Iraq, Afghanistan, Sudan, Yemen and now Ukraine? Will it help us to realize the European peace project[96], if we pursue the further development of the European Union into the status of a global political 'power" acting as a strong partner of NATO and as a

---

[96] It is not only on the website of the German government that the EU is called a peace project: https://www.bundesregierung.de/breg-de/schwerpunkte/europa/fragen-und-antworten-zu-frieden-in-europa-448742

"subject of the world politics of the future", as it is being sought by the EU under the leadership of France and Germany, together with other increasingly belligerent states, such as Poland and the Baltic countries?

As we have already mentioned above, in order to answer these questions, we must *move from the perception of symptoms to the understanding of reality*. This reality is hidden behind the veil of symptoms, which only show us a semblance of reality. We know reality is complex, but that shouldn't stop us from trying to understand it[97]. But how

---

[97] We quote Gerd Weidenhausen in Die Drei, No. 5., from a review by Wolfgang Bittner, "The Conquest of Europe by the USA", Mainz 2015, to illustrate how the European intelligentsia still falls for its own fear, and wants to present the matter as if the EU still had a choice, as if it still wanted to have a choice. It must be acknowledged: "The self-interest of the EU is the benefit of the USA". However, in our understanding, this is "over". It's done! The Europeans, especially the German intellectuals (the French are often still more courageous), instead of "acknowledging what is", still lose themselves in subjunctives out of fear. To put it clearly: The EU no longer pursues an independent policy, as any German Chancellor and Foreign Minister could confirm to us if he wanted to be honest. So here is the typical quote, in which it is pretended that the

should and can that work? As we have already said, the most important instrument for understanding is thinking, and the most important prerequisite is fearlessness in order to face the facts and the often terrible events, for which we humans are responsible[98].

So we want to name, at this stage, one simple fact that wants to hide behind the veil of symptoms and behind our fear of seeing

---

EU still has all options: "the tendency to appease the role of EU policy, which evolves in the wake of US policy: In its supposedly so noble democratization ambitions, the latter was not only thwarted or even betrayed by targeted US interventions within the framework of its "Eastern Neighborhood Policy", which has been practiced for some time, rather, it pursued very selfish economic and political interests from the outset, which made it forget to bring Russia on board in the negotiations on the EU Association Agreement with Ukraine. The mess that spread in the wake of this blatant omission was therefore, to a large extent, self-inflicted. Despite all the competition for influence and power, EU-Europe and the USA are pursuing a policy of division of labour with pre-distributed roles ...".

[98] This is how C. G. Jung expressed himself in his biography when he remarked, looking back on National Socialism and its consequences for Europe and the world: "If people had had the courage to look evil in the face and call it by its name, it could have been prevented".

things as they are. If one honestly reflects on the fact that China, measured by its large population, is a comparatively small country in terms of area and relatively poor in raw materials, then the thrust of the USA, with NATO as a transmission belt, quickly becomes apparent — if one has the courage and actually wants to understand. More on this on the next chapter.

THE APPROPRIATION OF RUSSIA'S RAW MATERIALS IS THE PREREQUISITE FOR POWER OVER CHINA[99]

The US pursues clear goals and long-term, strategic interests. You can't blame them for that. The long-term strategic goal of the American hegemonic strategy is to dominate the Chinese market, to shape it according to its own rules and "values". For the USA,

---

[99] Already in the Asia-Pacific-Forum of December 31, 2012, Noam Chomsky expressed himself on this topic in a clear and plausible way in an annual outlook. There he speaks of a "Revenge Of History: Chomsky On Japan, China, The United States, And The Threat of Conflict in Asia", i.e. of events that show how historical events can take revenge.

however, the path to dominance over China leads over the conquest of Russia. The US will therefore do everything it can to annex Russia's raw materials and natural resources via Europe.[100] Accepting this fact, we got to the root cause of the war in Ukraine, the regime change and unrest in Georgia and Armenia, and the other Caucasian countries.

Under the then Russian President Yeltsin[101], the USA already saw itself very close to its goal. They wanted to flood Russia with their capital, buy up the country and its resources and take it over "peacefully". Russia could have remained politically "independent", just like Germany and Europe. The economy and the financial industry dominating the country,

---

[100] A large number of analyses on the strategic orientation of American China policy can be found on the website of the Council on Foreign Relations (CFR), https://www.cfr.org/future-us-china-relations. Noam Chomsky also expressed himself in the spirit of our argumentation in a conversation with C. J. Polychroniou on the topic "Why China, not Russia, threatens the US-dominated world order". Published in German on July 9, 2022, in Telepolis; Original in Trouthout.

[101] From 1991 to 1999, Boris Yeltsin was the first president of Russia after the end of the Soviet Union.

however, would have been owned by and in the hands of Anglo-American capital and operated by it according to its rules.[102] Nor should it surprise anyone that the so-called "Russian crisis" that threatened the country in 1998 and 1999 was a debt crisis, the so-called "ruble crisis."[103] This debt would have provided an opportunity for foreign financial institutions and the Anglo-American financial cartels to take over the country's economy on favorable terms.[104] Local or regional investors

---

[102] This was a kind of "Rockefeller" capitalism that the US wanted to implement, regardless of the losses for Russia, and with a clear goal. During this time, the large private conglomerates of the oligarchs emerged. After 1999, Russia took back control over the most important conglomerates that were aiming to run the Russian economy, i.e. oil and gas companies, as well as the banks according to their own rules, and placed them under national supervision again. The trial against the oligarch Khodorkovsky was the last sensational act in this process so far.

[103] It is not unimportant to note here that the "Russian crisis" as an economic crisis began shortly after the beginning of the "Asian crisis". So it's a good time for global investors.

[104] Niall Ferguson shows very well in his book "Colossus" how the British already used the debt of states during their empire, examples are Iraq and Egypt, in order to be rewarded for their "effort", and to

in Russia, who had become nervous, sold their stocks, bonds and ruble holdings at low prices out of fear and transferred the proceeds to countries that seemed particularly safe, especially the UK and the USA. Russia was on the verge of bankruptcy.

The principle based and "natural" interest of US policy towards Russia at that time was therefore the complete takeover of its economic and natural resources, and this at the lowest possible price. The rest, areas such as culture and society, would not have been bothered by the USA. Culture in the USA has long been run by "media". In the long term, the Russians and their allies would also have watched mainly Hollywood films and communicated exclusively via the social media channels of American companies.

If the U.S. had succeeded in taking over Russia's economy and natural resources at that time, China's essential access to natural resources and raw materials would have been blocked in the future. The path to future growth would have been difficult, if not

---

bind the colonized states economically and financially to the British "motherland".

hindered, for the Chinese economy.[105] Without a reliable economic partnership with Russia, China would not have had the chance to match the American hegemon in the long term, or at least to fend it off. China would have had to pay the Anglo-American financial groups for the Russian raw materials. This is the "circular economy", the foreign policy, and the foreign trade "business model" that are guiding US hegemonic policy[106]. The United States, in possession of Russia's natural resources, would have become a hegemon without competition. It is exactly this hegemony that the United States is aiming for in the geopolitical global game of chess, an endeavor that has intensified since

---

[105] There is often talk about China's investments on the African continent. From this perspective, it should be clear that this is also primarily about raw materials and sales markets. From this point of view, the importance of Australia for China can also be understood. Australia has a relatively small population, but is in possession of large deposits of raw materials on its continent.

[106] So it is not out of pure suspicion to claim, that the US also earns money, when Saudi Arabia sells oil to China. This is a result of the still prevailing situation of the US-dominated global economic trade policy and geopolitics in . Details on this are given in our book on "War and Business", published in 2024 .

the end of the Cold War, as has been openly stated by Zbigniew Brzeziński, the advisor to several American presidents[107]. So this is "the crux of the matter". This is what the great global American strategy has been about since 1919, with Wilson's 14-points program for global peace, and with new intensity since 2001, with the "war against terror".

The growing intensity of this hegemonic striving is therefore essentially fed by two sources: on the one hand, from the increasing pressure from the exorbitantly growing and unsustainable American debt, and on the other hand, from the rise of China, as the first serious economic and political competitor that is considered by the USA as a future threat to their hegemonial position. This is the background to all the wars that have been waged recently by the United States and also by its proxies, from Afghanistan, as Pakistan's important neighbor, through Iran, Iraq, and from Syria over Libya to the poor country of Yemen, as guardian at the southern access to the Red Sea and the Suez Canal. In addition, since 2014, the USA and NATO have

---

[107] The Grand Chessboard: American Primacy and its Geostrategic Imperatives, by Zbigniew Brzezinski.

intensified the rearmament of Ukraine, with the clear goal of attacking Russia militarily. The open war that has been going on since 2022 can only be seen as a consequence of these developments. The smaller skirmishes, such as in Georgia and Armenia, we mention here only in passing. We also want to refrain from geopolitically important initiatives pushed forward by the USA and NATO in the Pacific, as we want to concentrate on Europe in this book.

So this is what is at stake on the chessboard for the American industry and capital: free access to raw materials and markets according to US rules and at favorable terms. These are the essential strategic elements. The African continent, as another large reservoir of raw materials, has a similar role to that of Russia, both overall and in the long term. However, the pressure to act there is not yet so great geostrategic.

For the USA, China is the great competitor that it wants to limit or, better said, "dominate" through Europe and the possession of Russia's raw materials and natural resources.

The industrial production capacities of Germany and Europe certainly also play an important role in this global strategy for hegemonial power, and could, of course, have played a role as an important collateral for Germany and for the other European countries. Germany, but also other European countries, still have good and very useful technical and industrial facilities, which, as we have seen, already belong to American owners, who can dispose of them largely at their will, if it really matters. In the event of war, as we are witnessing it in the context of the "war economy" that has been launched in Europe since 2023, Germany, together with the other European countries, will finally have to put their entire production capacities at the service of NATO, and thus at the service of the American geopolitical strategy. No German government has ever really left any doubt about this. Even the Green Foreign Minister Joschka Fischer was very diligent and sneaky in ideologically paving the way for the USA and NATO to southeastern Europe and the forceful destruction of Yugoslavia.[108] One

---

[108] Joschka Fischer's speech on the NATO mission in Kosovo and Serbia:

of the largest US military bases in Europe today is in Kosovo — which is not yet a nation, but is already an important pillar of the bridge to Eastern Europe and will, in the near future, for strategic geopolitical reasons, probably become a full member of the EU and NATO.

Just a small step further, one comes to the following statement: the EU and NATO are the bridge pillars of the USA in an easterly direction on the Eurasian continent in the struggle for global hegemony. In the west, i.e. the Pacific region, it is Japan and South Korea that had to take on the role of the US bridge pillars. The USA has not been pursuing an industrial location policy in Europe for a long time, but it is creating geostrategic facts to assert its own interests in the sense of the hegemony of Anglo-American capital and political power[109].

---

https://de.wikipedia.org/wiki/Rede_Joschka_Fischers_zum_NATO-Einsatz_im_Kosovo.

[109] On the close relationship between capital and war, see Niall Ferguson's books, for example: The Cash Nexus. Money and Power in the Modern World, 1700–2000, London: Allen Lane/Penguin Press, 2001; or: War of the World. History's Age of Hatred, 1914–1989, Allen

Since 1945 at the latest, Europe has progressively been incorporated and has no longer been considered a competitor to the USA, but an integral part of a global strategy for world domination. Already in the writings of Brzezinski, the European states are logically called "vassals".

BRIEF SUMMARY OF CHAPTER 1: THE REORGANIZATION OF THE WORLD AFTER VERSAILLES

Human history does not proceed like a mechanical construct, the world is too complex for that. And yet to the well-trained historian a certain direction and consistency in historical development become visible. Thus, we understand that certain decisions made in 1919 by the victorious powers of the First World War led to a new world order.

Looking at and analyzing the underlying principles that have been guiding the political

---

Lane, 2006. Niall Ferguson is certainly not a "revolutionary," but he is courageous, usually honest and extremely intelligent — a historian who can help us see the reality behind the symptoms. His specialty is the monetary and financial economy.

decision-makers, as well as the economic and financial managers in charge, provides us at the same time with a clear understanding of the processes that led to subsequent and current political and economic events and actions. The same principles that underpinned the decisions of that time during the "peace negotiations" can be seen at work during the processes of the shaping of power and domination that we have observed during the century following the Treaty of Versailles in 1919. This analytical work of the political and economic-trained historian is our way of recognizing a structure in the supposed chaos around us. Thus, our intention becomes evident that, with our book, we want to serve the process of learning from history.

The insights we have gained so far encourage us to take a close look again and again, when political decisions are made. We must face this challenge with attention and the awareness that the consequences of such decisions will have to be borne not only by us, but often even more so by the future inhabitants of this planet.

Chapter 7

How Europe Lost Her Identity: Taking Stock

INTRODUCTION

It is not our intention here to present a study on the integration process of the European Union (EU). It is rather our intention to show, on the basis of critical points and events, how this process has proceeded and to which important results it has led. The relationship between France and Germany after the Second World War and since the reunification of Germany and Europe after 1990, is at the heart of this part of our work. We will show how the relationship between the two economically and politically most important states in Europe, with the EU as the decisive shaping framework, has developed.

It is important for us to take a pan-European view, i.e. to see in the end, how Europe as a whole has developed geopolitically, and what scenario it presents to us today. At the same time, our attention is focused on the role of the USA, as the decisive co-shaping actor of the EU and as a critical influencing factor in the history of its emergence and specific organizational structuring.

BROTHERS UNDER ARMS 2019 – THE MEDIA WARNING SHOT

It was an article in the FAZ on the French National Day on July 14, 2019, that triggered us writing this section of our book. Please be reminded that this was exactly one hundred years after the signing of the Treaty of Versailles. In this article, the FAZ correspondent in France praised the new "brotherhood under arms" and underlined this importance with a picture showing French and German soldiers together at the parade in Paris on the Champs Elysées. We were immediately shocked by the presentation of this event, the joint parade of soldiers, as the most important symbol of German-French friendship in our time. The enthusiastic German comment on the picture reminded us of the public mood as it had been built up by political leaders in each of the two countries at the time of the "sleepwalkers" before the First World War. "Brothers in arms!" was the slogan in both countries before the outbreak of the First World War.[110] The title "Brothers under Arms!" is only minimally more nuanced.

If we had been shown a picture of German and French, as well as other European citizens, celebrating together on the Champs Elysées on 14 July, it could have made us happy, as a sign of international understanding and friendship. As it was, however, this lead story in the FAZ of 2019 was more like a media warning shot.

So we want to take this picture and the commentary in the FAZ as an opportunity to ask ourselves what distinguishes the relationship between France and Germany in particular, and in which direction it has developed over the past decades after World War II. We take the EU as a kind of overarching political framework to draw the lessons from the development of the relationship between these two countries. We will find out at the end of this chapter that the

---

[110] At the same time, France has also financed the armament of Russia and Serbia through its banks, especially Rothschild, in order to prepare the two-front war. see "The Sleepwalkers: How Europe Went into the First World War", Christopher Clark, DVA, 2013.

evolution of the "French-German Friendship" has had a significant impact on Europe as a whole.

THE FOUNDING YEARS OF THE EU: CENTRAL STATE OR COMMUNITY OF FATHERLANDS?

Since the first steps towards the founding of the EU in the early 1950s, through the European Coal and Steel Community (ECSC) to the Treaties of Rome, which were signed in 1957 by the six founding states[111] to establish the European Economic Community (EEC), these European states have agreed in principle to draw lessons from the wars of the past in order to shape the future within the framework of a European community that lives and works together peacefully. In addition to the European victorious powers of the Second World War, i.e. France and England, the USA also emphatically supported this process of European unification from the very beginning.

---

[111] The six founding countries are France, Germany, Italy, Belgium, the Netherlands and Luxembourg.

It is remarkable, however, that two fundamentally different political tendencies became noticeable right from the start. On the one hand, there was France, which is considered in Europe to be the first historically grown central state[112], and which did not want to give up its role as a "Grande Nation", strove for a confederation of states. In contrast, the USA, which took its own federal state as the most appropriate model, supported the formation of a European central and unitary state since the first years of European unification. The creation of such a federal state, based on the American model, would have meant that the previously sovereign European nation states relinquish their sovereignty and delegate most of their sovereign power to the European central state.[113]

---

[112] On this by Fernand Braudel, l'Identité de la France. Published in German as "France, Volume 1: Space and History / Volume 2: The People and the Things / Volume 3: The Things and the People, 2009, Fernand Braudel.
[113] We will mention here only one book by Frederic Bozo that deals with this issue, "Deux stratégies pour l'Europe", Paris, 1996.

In a third group, Switzerland, England, Norway, Sweden, Austria, Portugal and Denmark founded the European Free Trade Association (EFTA) in 1960, which from the outset was explicitly and essentially limited to the freedom of trade and the movement of goods, but left the political sovereign power of action to the individual countries as independent nations.

So there was an obvious contradiction, on the one hand between the model of a European central and unitary state according to the aspirations of the USA, and on the other hand the model of a federalist confederation of states, as it is still implemented today by EFTA.[114]

In concrete terms, this historic European integration process showed very early on that the USA, as a kind of regulatory power, was pursuing very concrete goals in Europe.[115]

---

[114] The European Free Trade Area, founded in 1960, currently comprises only the four states of Iceland, Liechtenstein, Norway and Switzerland.

[115] We refer the reader for more details on these processes and the determining role of the USA to Eckart Conze: Die gaullistische Herausforderung. Die Deutsch-Französischen Beziehungen in der

Thus, under pressure from the USA and through the skills of their French lobbyist, Jean Monnet, the USA succeeded in limiting the effectiveness and scope of EFTA. The EFTA founding states, England, Austria, Denmark and Sweden were soon forced under pressure from the USA to switch to the camp of the EEC and the later EU.[116] In this way, the US achieved a greater uniformity to facilitate their political, economic and trade relations with the EU and, in their eyes, make it more efficient. More importantly, however, the US saw the EU as an integral part of NATO from the outset. The economic and military zones of influence should therefore be increasingly centralized in a coherent manner.[117]

---

amerikanischen Europapolitik 1958–1963, Munich, 1995.

[116] Of course, we have to see the Brexit of 2020 in this context. In the long run, England does not want to be integrated into a centralist confederation of states in order to give up its sovereignty there.

[117] At this point, we should not forget that the European states, especially the victorious powers England and France, but also Italy, were heavily dependent on the USA and had to repay loans they

This centralist approach of the EU, demanded by the United States and skillfully promoted by Jean Monnet at the political level, was soon opposed in France by General de Gaulle, who had become the first president of the Fifth Republic in 1959, under the constitutional reform formulated under his leadership. De Gaulle, as President of France, ended the war in Algeria and also successively granted independence to the other French colonies. De Gaulle was personally convinced of the necessity of building the process of European unification on the basis of the identity of historically grown cultural, social and political individual European countries. Only through a healthy national and cultural identity of the nations in Europe could, in his understanding, a freely willed union of the European states function in the long term.

---

had taken out during the war years in the first decades to lead the fight against the Nazi regime.

The Marshall Plan was launched for Germany, which very quickly and successfully strengthened economic relations between Germany and the USA and led to close integration of the two economies at an early stage, with Germany as the junior partner.

This phase of European integration after 1945 and up to 1963 has been analyzed in detail by the German historian Eckart Conze and presented in various studies and books. Conze presented a first detailed study of the American policy towards German-French relations in the period of 1949 to 1963, under the title "The Gaullist Challenge", as early as 1995[118]. In it, Conze writes in the first lines of Chapter II: "Research rightly and almost unanimously considers the USA to be the hegemonic power of the Western world since 1945", and further down "The Second World War had a catalytic function for the emergence of American hegemony". Conze also confirms that the Americans striving for hegemony had a "triple interest in European unification", because although it was "primarily economic", it was also "thought through from the beginning, militarly and politically". In our context, Conze's assessment is that "the supranational

---

[118] Eckart Conze: Hegemony through Integration: The American European Policy and its Challenge by de Gaulle, in: Institut für Zeitgeschichte, Vierteljahreshefte für Zeitgeschichte, Volume 43 (1995), Issue 2.

integration approach of the Treaties of Rome ... also aimed at the establishment of supranational political structures" in the medium term. He goes on to state that "de Gaulle's conception of Europe, the center of which was the national sovereignty of the individual states", contradicted this.

General de Gaulle was considered by all sides undoubtedly a convinced European. He vigorously pursued, from the onset, reconciliation with the newly formed Federal Republic of Germany. This was in line with the great importance he attached to the sovereignty of the nation-states in Europe. In 1963, de Gaulle and Adenauer signed the Élysée Treaty in Paris, the so-called Franco-German Friendship Treaty, which since then has promoted relations between the two countries, building on regular consultations and various measures to strengthen mutual trust and cooperation. De Gaulle wanted to recognize Germany's national sovereignty through this act and give it special emphasis. Only sovereign nations, in de Gaulle's eyes, could be sovereign political and economic partners.

In this sense, France, under President de Gaulle, soon changed its policy toward NATO. From the outset, the US had rejected the French proposal for a European army under French leadership and with the inclusion of Germany. After France had succeeded in rapidly building up its nuclear force, the *Force de frappe,* since 1960, and especially after de Gaulle's re-election in 1965, France intensified her efforts to form a European defense policy independent of the United States. France wanted to continue to play an active role in shaping NATO, but with an independent European defense alliance, as part of NATO. NATO was to be brought under European command in Europe, and the American and Canadian troops were to be placed under European command. The US categorically rejected this request, whereupon de Gaulle demanded the withdrawal of Allied troops and NATO headquarters from France. Since 1966 at the latest, de Gaulle justified this attitude with a clear political assessment, announcing that "France is now striving for the full exercise of its sovereignty, which cannot be guaranteed by the stationing of foreign forces on its soil".[119] At the same time, de Gaulle declared the withdrawal of French troops from NATO, where they were under American command. The 30,000 NATO soldiers had to leave France, and the various NATO military quarters and command centers were moved to Belgium, the Netherlands and Germany.

THE COMPLEMENTARY STARTING POSITION OF GERMANY AND FRANCE: GERMANY'S UNCONDITIONAL ORIENTATION TOWARDS THE WEST AND FRANCE'S CLAIM TO A LEADING ROLE IN EUROPE

As we have seen, there were two fundamentally different ideas and visions for the European Union and about its future political design. The first, and prioritized, idea was favored by the Americans and, in the

---

[119] We read about this in Der Spiegel, 14.03.1966, "France – US bases – ground, sky, sea. - In 1944, the Americans came to liberate de Gaulle's France. In 1966, de Gaulle wants to liberate France from the Americans."

person of Jean Monnet, promoted[120] within the power structures in Europe to promote the American incorporation of Europe. This concept of the structure and organization of the EU worked towards a federal state, as a centralized unitary state, in which individual nations would gradually transfer their national powers to the EU and delegate them to her responsibility. The second vision is closely linked to the person of General de Gaulle, who vigorously defended this position in Europe and the political ideas associated with it. This idea is based on the emphasis on a strong position of the sovereign states and strives for a confederation of states of the "fatherlands". According to this model,

---

[120] We refer here to the excellent analysis by Werner Wüthrich, who dealt in detail with the topic of "European integration" in the Swiss magazine ' Zeit-Fragen" from 2011 to 2012. There he also presents the "Monnet method" as the key to understanding the Euro crisis. In other articles, he shows in a historical context the two fundamentally different approaches to organizing the countries of Europe – the concept of the European Community and that of EFTA, the European Free Trade Association. In doing so, he also works very well on the underlying political principles of these two concepts, one of which is more centralist and the other federalist.

nations should agree on common goals, such as the creation of a common market and a common defense. However, the basis and principled actors of cooperation should always be the individual, sovereign states. [121]

On paper, i.e. according to the theory, this organizational structure of the EU as a confederation of states was valid for a long time. In principle, it still is today. The European Commission is the "guardian of the Treaties" and, in principle, has no executive function. In principle, it must follow the guidelines and implement the decisions of the national governments, the Council of the European Union. In reality, these intentions could not prevail. This is shown very convincingly by Charles B. Blankart in his studies and books, in which he assumes the importance of the "financial constitution" in the European Union, i.e. the power over the finances of the EU structures. He emphatically shows, how the "paradigm shift

---

[121] In an interview published in GlobalBridge on May 21, 2024, British historian and Russia expert Richard Sakwa also takes this position, calling himself a "Gaullist." We are at the funeral of the old school of diplomacy", on May 21, 2024.

in European, and especially in German federalism after the First World War," prevailed. Blankart makes it clear that federalism in its current form no longer has a future within the European Union. This is due to structural reasons linked to the "financial constitution" of the European Union. The centralized unitary state has become a reality for the European Union.

Under Commission President Ursula von der Leyen, this development toward the unitary and central state of the EU has finally been rooted in the practice of cooperation between the EU institutions, first under the pretext of the measures taken during the so-called Corona pandemic and finally in the post-2022 period, since the war in Ukraine. Already under the reign of the German Chancellor Angela Merkel, competences and functions were increasingly and systematically delegated to the European Commission. The German Chancellor benefited from the fact that during her long reign[122], in France, the French presidency was held by Nicola Sarkozy, Francois Holland and Emmanuel

---

[122] She was Chancellor from 22 November 2005 to 8 December 2021.

Macron, rather weak or even insignificant political figures. With the current presidency of the European Commission, Ursula von der Leyen, a politician protégé of Merkel, came into play and was enthroned in 2019. She has vehemently pursued the transatlantic policies of Germany, represents the absolute and exclusive Western orientation of European politics, and is willing to enforce this policy ruthlessly for the entire EU without any restraint.

This principle based attitude of closely aligning the EU with US policy had increasingly become evident during the Corona policy, when the Commission President awarded large contracts to US pharmaceutical companies "freehand".[123] Recently, this unilateral position of the EU has deepened, not least under the uncompromising commitment to NATO policy and the massive provision of arms and financial resources to Ukraine. Effective, or

---

[123] To this end, lawsuits, including by EU member states, were filed in European courts against Ms von der Leyen's behavior in May 2024. The hearings were then adjourned by Belgian courts for unknown reasons.

even critical control by the member states, is being perceived less and less, and in some cases, as in the case of Hungary, even sanctioned. The member states were brought into line. The docile behavior of Member States that have serious economic and financial problems, such as Italy, France and Greece, has been ensured by the creation of new instruments facilitating the generous allocation of enormous financial resources to graciously honor their political alignment and support with economic and financial boons. The massive and targeted provision of funding for public relations work and the media ensured general approval among the general public in Europe. Critical voices were increasingly prevented by laws, decrees and regulations to be classified as "endangering the system" or anti-democratic[124]. The European Commission (EC) has thus put herself in a position, in which it has "ruled

---

[124] There is now a "Democracy Promotion Act" in the EU. Regarding the laws, if you issue orders to prevent public opinion, it is sufficient to obtain information from the press reports on the control of social media and the public media (ÖRR). Censorship by so-called "Corrective" institutes, which are funded by the state, speaks for itself.

through" since the Corona policy and the war in Ukraine[125], i.e. without perceptible control by the populations of the member states, announcing its decisions or pushing them through according to its ideas and those of the leaders in the most important member states. In this way, the European Commission (EC) has managed to get the right from the EU Member States to leverage her financial resources by taking debt on its own, i.e. by bringing its own bonds onto the market, controlled by institutions under the supervision of the European Commission and secured by the member states[126]. Even a brief critical look at these processes will show any observer that these processes of institutionalization and centralization of the EU have become irreversible.

---

[125] "Governing through" was a wish formula of the German Chancellor for the design of political processes; i.e. governing without obstacles. In the daily newspaper "Die Welt" of 07.04.2010, the report "Merkel says goodbye to "governing through". Was that the case?

[126] Prof. Hans-Werner Sinn, former director of the IFO-Institute in Munich, has followed these developments most consistently.

In the following paragraphs, we would like to take a further look at how the EU has developed historically, and which path of development the EU has taken in concrete terms. In this overview, we want to limit ourselves to the two states that were considered decisive for structuring the EU, i.e. France and Germany. Of course, we will always keep an eye on the role and influence of the United States through NATO, but also through its dominant economic power over Europe. At the end of this analytical overview, we will look at the current situation in order to see where we stand today in this process of European unification, what the consequences of the past European unification and integration policy have been for both countries, and finally, we will ask what possible options for shaping politics in Europe still exist in the future.[127]

---

[127] At this point, we will not go into the Marshall Plan, whose economic importance of which is usually greatly overestimated. Its main importance lies in its promotion of European integration in accordance with the will of the United States. S. h. Hans-Werner Sinn: "Der Mythos vom Marshall-Plan"; as well as the economic historian Werner Abelshauser, who in his books on the "Myth of the Economic Miracle" also

For Germany, the consistent West-oriented orientation of politics is[128] an outstanding and consistent feature that has become formative since 1949, under the government of Konrad Adenauer, to today's governments, not only for German foreign policy, but also for its consistent and narrow economic and political ties to the USA. Even minor frictions or major public debates in the meantime do not change anything on this position. The transatlantic network[129] has done excellent

---

refutes the thesis of the "initial spark" of the Marshall Plan.

[128] The orientation towards the West was implemented in the interests of the USA through Western integration. It should be noted, however, that Germany is still subject to certain restrictions on sovereignty and has not received a peace treaty from the victorious powers of the time to this day. In the "special case", the USA can therefore determine war and peace in Germany to this day. In today's public discussion and reporting, this is called the "trans-Atlantic relationship": https://www.swp-berlin.org/themen/dossiers/die-usa-und-die-transatlantischen-beziehungen

[129] "Expanding and strengthening the transatlantic network" is a consistent demand of the German government. https://www.bundesregierung.de/breg-de/service/bulletin/das-transatlantische-netzwerk-ausbauen-und-verstaerken-rede-des-bundeskanzlers-

work for decades to effectively assert its interests. This political orientation towards the West, which is most clearly expressed by Germany's early rearmament and integration into NATO, was further strengthened by the close and steadily growing economic ties with the USA[130]. Over the decades, especially after 1949, an increasingly close-knit interdependence has developed in the areas of economics and finance.

For France, the situation was different from the beginning. We recall here that France was only subsequently accepted by the Allies as a victorious power of the Second World War and was granted her own occupation zone in the South-West of Germany. For France under General de Gaulle, it was clear that it deserved and had to have a place as a sovereign European nation at the table of the

---

in-chicago-804836.Eine good source is Stefan Fröhlich, "The Transatlantic Relations", Germany, 2017 as a lobby organization of European and American corporations and business associations, which was created to influence cooperation between Europe, the EU and the USA.

[130] The economic interdependence had existed since the 1920s. It was then further intensified after 1945 by the Marshall Plan.

great nations. Even early and targeted efforts by certain political and economic circles in France, which advocated for close political and economic ties with the USA, cannot deny this political stance for an independent position of France promoted by de Gaulle.[131] For France after the Second World War, the claim to be a "Grande Nation", a country that had to have its legitimate place among the great nations in the world, remained part of her historical profile. Of course, this claim is also fed by the strong cultural charisma of France, which was so dominant in Europe for a long time, that the educated circles from Paris to Berlin, Warsaw and Petersburg spoke and thought French.[132]

We will show that this different starting position of the two nations, France and

---

[131]. We refer here to the study on the "History of the EU – Part 1, in Zeit-Fragen, No. 38, 2010.

[132] We remember Walter Benjamin, who called Paris the "capital of the 19th century".
Even a man like Alexander von Humboldt, who could not have been more Prussian in terms of his constitution, preferred to spend time either in nature, travelling, or in Paris. Even Napoleon and his soldiers were able to converse in French throughout their war in Russia.

Germany, is also reflected in the particular processes of European unification and integration, as well as in the results that these processes have brought for the respective countries.

THE "EUROPEAN AXIAL AGE" OF 1985-95 UNDER DELORS AND MITTERRAND

The period after 1985, when Jacques Delors began to serve as President of the European Commission, started still during the period of the EEC before the formal establishment of the EU. This period is considered to be the decisive phase in the shaping of the EU. Delors had been promoted to this post by the French President François Mitterrand, where he gave proof of his exceptional political expertise from 1985 to 1995. Delors had represented France in the European Parliament early on, and then distinguished himself as an outstanding and loyal politician in several governments under Mitterrand's presidency. This period of European integration under the Mitterrand-Delors axis constituted, in retrospect and in several respects, the "European Axial Period", during which the policies of European unification and integration, as well as France's role in Europe and as a global power, changed fundamentally. As we will see, both events are again strongly related to the parallel expansion of American dominance in Europe.

In the literature on this topic, reference is usually made to the fact that since the 1980s and then also through the new constellation after the reunification of the two German states and the collapse of the Soviet confederation, Delors had strived for and promoted an ever greater deepening of the integration of the European states in the EU. This indicates, it is assumed, that Delors and Mitterrand worked towards the European, centralist federal state. Superficially, this assumption is certainly correct and overall indisputable. However, this assumption deserves a more nuanced consideration. This view does not automatically mean that Delors and Mitterrand also sought the realization of the European federal state under US hegemony. On the contrary, the intention was driven by a strong primacy for European interests. Neither Mitterrand nor Delors would deny this; rather, this attitude has been at the core of their political life. We must not overlook the fact that France's goal was to establish her role as a major European power through the EU and, if possible, to promote this role even further.

For both politicians, France's Gaullist claim to recognition as an equal partner of the great nations was non-negotiable. In this sense, Mitterrand and Delors were staunch nationalists and Gaullists. In this sense, European integration was to be primarily oriented towards the interests of France and the EU was to be shaped according to the still prevailing statist ideas of the French bureaucracy. Under these premises, both politicians strove for a European Union that would become a mixture of a centralist-federalist state, but at the same time be able to assert its claims on the international stage in a sovereign manner vis-à-vis foreign powers, especially the United States. It is in this spirit that all of Delors' work as President of the European Commission should be understood.

As early as 1986, under Delors as President of the EEC, the Treaty of Rome of 1957 was sustainably reformed for the first time and the foundations for the European internal market were laid. To this end, the "Delors Commission", created for this purpose, developed the mechanism of the European legislative process, which has remained the valid "benchmark" and formal guide to this day, in an extended form via the "acquis communautaire"[133], for the proceedings for integration and association of other member and partner countries. Since then, this formal integration process does not only concern the structuring of the internal market, but all areas of public life are included without exception, from the rule of law, trade, economic rules and laws, as well as social norms and the media, and not to forget migration and foreign policy. This far-reaching process of legal and regulatory unification of the countries of Europe and the associated states had been legally adopted by 1992 and the results had become legally valid from 1993 onwards as part of the mutual obligations of the member states. The EU was thus finally established as a construct

---

[133] In legal jargon, this is called the "EU acquis".

based on the rule of law.[134] This must be highlighted as the first major achievement of the European Commission under Delors.

In parallel with this process, and in consistent complement to it, Delors presented a three-stage plan for the establishment of the Economic and Monetary Union in 1989. He had asked the European Council, i.e. the European member states, to provide him with the mandate for this initiative, which he had initiated, as early as 1988. The work of the Delors Commission was presented to the European Council in a report which then became the basis for the development of Economic and Monetary Union through the Maastricht Treaty[135], which is now regarded as the founding act of the European Union. This result from 1993 is considered the

---

[134]This process is fully documented and described on the official website of the EU under https://Europa.eu/.
[135] It should be noted here that the most important demand of France, represented by Mitterrand, during the negotiations on German reunification, was the abandonment of the Deutsche Mark and the adoption of the Euro as the future European currency. France thus saw itself as an active participant in Germany's economic potential.

outstanding achievement under the EU Commission of Delors.

THE TURNING POINT IN THE PROCESS OF EUROPEAN INTEGRATION AND THE END OF THE "GRANDE NATION"

However, here we come to a crucial point in our argumentation. For what at first glance looks like a great moment for the future of France and her European, but also her global political claims, ultimately becomes the decisive turning point in the French history. In the sense *of an irony of history*[136], the end of the "Grande Nation" is looming from this point on. The key to this understanding can be found, if we take a closer look at the role of the United States in this process.

We should not assume that the US played with hidden cards during this time. Rather, it seemed to have been a game with an open

---

[136] In the social sciences and humanities, the principle of "unintended consequences" or "unintended effects" has been known for a long time.
https://de.wikipedia.org/wiki/Unbeabsichtigte_Folgen#cite_note-1.

outcome. Measured against the hegemonic importance that the USA had achieved economically and militarily after the Second World War, however, the outcome should no longer be surprising. As we shall see, the process of European integration led to the result that the United States has sought from the beginning. European integration followed along the lines the United States have wished and worked for since 1945, and, ironically, it also provoked the end of France as the "Grande Nation".

French politics has reached a point, from which it would only have made progress on the desired nationalist path through a consistent continuation of politics in the sense of the Gaullist-formulated interests of the French nation. However, history wanted it differently, and the course of history led to a different result. Delors and Mitterrand retired in 1994 and 1995 as key figures in shaping French and EU policies[137]. This did not ensure a consistent continuation on the federalist

---

[137] Mitterrand stepped down from the French political scene in 1995 after his second mandate. He died in 1996 and ended his EU presidency in 1994 after three terms in office.

path initiated by the EU under the leadership of France and was ultimately gambled away for France, as we will briefly show here in the following part of our descriptive analysis.

At first glance, it looks as if France has obviously taken on the dominant role in the policy of European integration during the three terms of Delors' EU presidency. It seemed as if France had been able to clearly defend her interests and achieved her major goals. It seemed quite clear that with the implementation of the 3-step plan of the European Commission under the leadership of Delors and under the Treaty of Maastricht, the European Union would finally have a French face, a French structure and a French intellectual and political leadership. But this appearance is deceptive.

For the preservation and consistent enforcement of French interests would have required at the same time a defense against the Americanization of European politics[138].

---

[138] For an introduction to the topic, we recommend by Anselm Doering-Manteuffel, Amerikanisierung und Westernisierung, Version: 2.0, in: Docupedia-Zeitgeschichte, 19.08.2019.

However, it turned out that even political great leaders like Mitterrand and Delors were not up to the challenge in the end. The reason for this is very easy to find in Germany's particular geopolitical position. American policy towards European unification has been consistent and unambiguous. The position of Germany, which was economically integrated and dominated by the USA from the beginning, and was severely limited in its political maneuverability as a nation by unconditional loyalty to the USA and NATO, was decisive for the achievement of the American political goals in Europe. In Europe, France was thus largely alone with its original policy of centralist-federalist confederation of states, according to Gaullist ideas and under French leadership, in contrast to the model of the centralist federal state promoted by the USA.[139]

---

[139] The USA knew very early on how to bring England, Austria and Denmark into line, i.e. away from EFTA and towards the emerging EU.

Werner Wüthrich shows this process in great detail and convincingly in a series of several articles in the Swiss magazine "Zeit-Fragen" under the title "European Integration".

Mitterrand and Delors were always realistic enough to assume that the European integration process would largely follow Monnet's[140] ideas and would follow the example of the USA towards a European federal state. Mitterrand was an excellent realpolitiker, who consistently pursued his goals, but at the same time, did not refuse to accept political constraints and facts. Mitterrand and Delors therefore knew that, in the very end, they could not assume that the United States would allow the trump cards it had in the form of dominance over Germany and NATO to be taken out of their hands.

There he also goes into great detail and knowledge of the different roles of Jean Monnet and de Gaulle.

A convincing analysis of the influence of the USA on the process of European unification was presented by the German historian Andreas Bracher in his book "Europe in the American World System, Fragments of an Unwritten History of the 20th Century", Basel, 2001.

[140] Let us remind you that Jean Monnet and Robert Schumann are usually referred to together as the founding fathers of the European Union. it does not mention that the positions of the two politicians were very different. Monnet clearly pursued the policy of forming a European nation-state, while Schumann favored the Gaullist "Europe of the Fatherlands".

However, as staunch Gaullists, they did everything in their power and hoped to the end that this centralist European federal state would ultimately be under the clear leadership of France. France was to play the leading role in preserving European sovereignty and the power to shape[141] European politics.[142] That is why I have adopted this paradoxical designation of Mitterrand and Delors as "Gaullists", while both belonged to the French Socialist Party and were not formally classified as Gaullists in

---

[141] The article by Günther Hellmann in the series "From Politics and Contemporary History" on the topic "Between creative power and hegemony trap. On the latest debate on a "new German foreign policy", very worth reading. It should be noted here that in these discussions a distinction is made between decision-making power and creative power.

[142] In this context, it is important to point out that in 2010 Delors was instrumental in the creation of the "Spinelli Group", which was founded as an initiative of the European Parliament to promote efforts within the EU to create a federalist confederation.

It should also not be forgotten that Delors was probably the last president in the EU who convincingly represented the principle of "subsidiarity" and emphasized its importance for shaping European policy.

France[143]. In their politics, however, both were convinced Gaullists, i.e. French nationalists. When we speak here of French leadership and political creative power, we mean spiritual orientation and political leadership by the national genius of France[144]. The leadership of France in Europe was not going to be realized. Europe had finally become prey to the American hunger for power and money, the key ingredients in its struggle for global hegemony. What started after 1945, as hegemonial power over the "West", would progressively strive to cover the entire planet, as we may wish to thoroughly understand through the reading of our book on "War and Business", published in August 2024.

---

[143] In the "normal" French understanding of politics, socialist politicians are not Gaullists, because according to this understanding they should belong to the conservative party.
But we call Mitterrand and Delors Gaullists here because they represented de Gaulle's policy, that is, a policy that always keeps an eye on France's national interests as a "Grande Nation" and must never give up.
[144]

https://fr.wikipedia.org/wiki/G%C3%A9nie_fran%C3%A7ais

To achieve this goal of French supremacy over Germany and over Europe, the French saw the need for the German economic capacities and resources to be transferred to the EU. Hence, Mitterrand's *bon mot* that he did not desire anything from the Germans as much as the Deutsche Mark and the Deutsche Bundesbank. In fact, France under Mitterrand prevailed in the negotiations for German unity after 1989 and had the currency unit and the Euro fixed as an equivalent for its approval of German reunification. These results of the negotiations on reunification were then consistently implemented in the Maastricht Treaty under the leadership of Delors. Politically, of course, the Bundesbank has nothing directly to do with German unity. Strategically, however, the takeover of the Deutsche Bundesbank by abandoning the Deutsche Mark and introducing the Euro was the decisive step in transferring control of the country's economic capacities and financial resources to the EU under French leadership. From the point of view of Mitterrand and Delors, this was tantamount to placing the German industrial capacities and resources under French supervision and control within the EU. [145]

In summary, we have to say that Mitterrand's policy was always very realistic, but at the same time strategically clever and long-term. In doing so, he always kept in mind that it must be the goal of French politics to secure the "Grande Nation" its legitimate place among the nations. However, Mitterrand could not overlook the fact that the United States, as a consequence of the outcome of the Second World War, was striving for a hegemony through the creation of a new world order, which was based on the institutions of Bretton Woods and the UN Security Council. In the eyes of Mitterand, the European policy of the US with their predominant influence in Europe could have been contained by a united Europe, with France and Germany at the center. According

---

[145] This was a decisive step forward in the complete takeover of Germany by France, as it had been pursued and claimed in the Treaty of Versailles under Clemenceau. In part of the German public, this result of European integration is also called "Versailles 2.0". The article in Telepolis, "Complete, legal expropriation by law", by Marc Friedrich and Matthias Weik, 2019, is worth reading.

to this understanding, France needed the EU, with Germany as the dominant economic power, in order to be able to assert her place as the "Grande Nation" against the hegemony of the USA. Mitterrand took over this claim of France's important role from de Gaulle.[146] According to France's ideas, i.e. the ideas of Mitterand, the basic structure of the EU was to be shaped in such a way that, in conjunction with Germany's economic power, it would play a sovereign role in world politics. In this sense, France and her policy under Mitterrand and Delors was the final attempt to establish the bulwark against US hegemony in Europe. As we understand today, this bulwark has completely collapsed.

France has to admit that since 2022 at the latest, with Ukraine and Europe's proxy war against Russia, the US has emerged as the clear winner from these European developments for integration. The big loser in particular is France, which has finally been

---

[146] Refer to François Mitterrand: un socialiste Gaullien, T. Desjardins, Paris, Hachette 1978 ; or the biography "C'était François Mitterrand", by Jacques Attali, Paris, 2007, a long-time companion and confidant of Mitterand.

downgraded to the second rank of the nations. Certainly, there have always been other EU states that would have liked to see an independent and sovereign European policy, such as Denmark, Austria, the Netherlands or the Czech Republic. However, Germany in particular could not and did not want to free itself from the economic and security clutches of the USA and NATO. Realistically, it was practically impossible for Germany to achieve a truly sovereign status after 1949.[147]

The Treaty of Maastricht, signed in 1993, thus created the EU as the decisive stage in the realization of an "ever closer union of the peoples of Europe", as the treaty itself says. France had not succeeded in consolidating its dominance in Europe, because the crucial partner France needed for this model of a sovereign EU had long since ceased to be independent. Germany was, to put it in the language of the United States, a loyal vassal

---

[147] It is known that the victorious powers of the Second World War have not yet offered Germany a peace treaty.

on the great chessboard of American hegemonic claim in Europe.[148]

And yet, we may ask ourselves: Why should we not want to live under this constellation in Europe? After all, it is true that since 1949, we have been able to lead a largely peaceful life in Europe, which has gone hand in hand with unprecedented prosperity and wealth. Isn't this call for European sovereignty a nostalgic undertaking, without concrete, urgent justification and ultimately directed against the interests of the EU itself? – These questions are certainly justified and deserve analytical consideration in the sense of a current assessment. We would like to make a contribution to this here afterward in the following chapters.

---

[148] This assessment is consistently used in the publications of the Foreign Policy Research Institute in the United States and is supported by the book "The Grand Chessboard: American Primacy and its Geostrategic Imperatives", by Zbigniew Brzezinski, New York, Basic Books, 1997.

EUROPE LOSING HER WAY - GOING ASTRAY ON AMERICAN PATHS

With the intention of reflecting on our own interests and the necessary positioning of France, Germany and the EU on the map we are drawing, we would like to return briefly to the "brothers in arms" marching in 2019 together on the Champs-Élysées. This image, which we have pointed out in the introduction to this chapter, does not want to get out of our heads anymore.

We agree that this image is not the only one that is symptomatic of the EU and the common policy of France and Germany. We do not overlook the most valuable circumstances of an open borders policy and the results of economic integration by the EU. However, the question must be asked again and again as to who determines the rules according to which we want to shape life in Europe. This is, if you like, the 'primal question' that de Gaulle posed very clearly and emphatically, and which we should ask ourselves again today. After all, the demands of the Declaration of Human Rights for freedom, equality and fraternity do not only apply to individuals, but they must also apply to states and countries, where this is called the "right of self-determination" or sovereignty. Countries and the people who live in them must have the right to self-determination and to the self-determined shaping of their respective communities.[149]

---

[149] We subliminally ask the question of the "raison d'être", a term that is kept directly out of all discussions in Germany with reference to the Basic Law.

We, on the other hand, are of the opinion that the "raison d'état", i.e. the question of the meaning of our state, must be asked anew.

The ruling parties obviously see the reason of the state in gaining ever greater international prestige and greater power by generating more and more funds, which are then available for "international tasks" in the sense of NATO, the EU and the UN, as well as to raise the egoistic profile of the international power elites.

It is time to fundamentally change this understanding of raison d'être, which was essentially coined by Machiavelli and other contemporaries during the Renaissance.

We see the fundamental raison d'être in securing and, if possible, expanding prosperity and quality of life for the population. "Power" is only the decisive factor in a hostile environment. In a world of cooperation, "power" becomes secondary.

Since 1919, the U.S., under its President Wilson, has introduced the international doctrine of interference in the affairs of foreign states on the world stage as a legitimate instrument of power in global politics. Since then, a country can also be punished by means of violence and war, or sanctioned, if the dominant power is of the opinion that a country does not abide by rules set by the dominant power.[150] This Wilsonianism, then, is not primarily about a contest of better ideas, but it derives its "right" and even its "duty" to interfere from the American self-image, that is, the way the American people see their "missionary" destiny. In this sense, NATO then also became an "alliance of values", [151]i.e. a military instrument to put the "missionary" destiny of the USA into practice. This

---

[150] Niall Ferguson described and traced this "imperialism" in great detail in its historical development and in its various shades in his book "Colossus: The Rise and Fall of the American Empire", 2004.

[151] In line with our argumentation, Sevim Dağdelen has recently published a comprehensive book "NATO: A Reckoning with the Alliance of Values", 2024.

missionary "value imperialism"[152] explicitly involves the interference and violent correction of the political behavior of countries, today officially called "regime change," as well as the instrument of sanctions, which have become a popular tool of American politics today.[153] It has turned out for the USA that this instrument

---

[152] We also refer here to the "Series: Dresden Collected Comments on Security Policy – dgksp discussion papers – of 14 April 2021.

[153] see "Extraterritorial US sanctions", by Sascha Lohmann, in SWP-Aktuell 2019/A 31, May 2019. - In it, he writes: "Since the founding of the republic, the US government has been expanding its authority beyond its own borders to pursue economic, foreign and security policy goals. The extraterritorial application of U.S. law to natural and legal persons, assets and actions outside one's own territory is favored by three factors: First, by an ideological obligation to a natural right, which is expressed in a commitment to the inviolability of inalienable rights that are considered valid even beyond one's own borders. Secondly, by a legal culture that is characterized by the experience of constant territorial expansion and domination – initially as a former settler society and later as an occupying power after the Second World War. And third, through an independent judiciary that has a wide margin of discretion to interpret the geographic scope of U.S. law and its enforcement by administrative authorities."

of sanctions, due to the exclusive American power of disposal over powerful instruments for financial transactions,[154] together with its dominant role as an economic power, can be used in a targeted and effective manner for the interests of the USA[155]. Such sanctions are increasingly applied by the US jointly with their partners from the EU, Canada and Japan in order to influence the economic well-being of entire countries and their populations in a targeted manner and also to hit them economically by force.[156]

---

[154] Refer to the excellent article "The Super Weapon of Mr. Glaser, Sanctions against Russia and Iran: How American Tax Officials Become Economic Warriors", by Kerstin Kohlenberg and Mark Schieritz, on October 23, 2014, in DIE ZEIT No. 44/2014.

[155] In the war against Russia that is currently being waged in Ukraine, it has become clear that the US is using the sanctions policy against Russia for its own interests. In the case of Nordstream 2, this went so far that an important infrastructure for Europe's energy supply was blown up in order to promote the American energy industry.

[156] As we write this text, hundreds of sanctions are being applied by the US, particularly against North Korea, Iran, Syria, Venezuela, Russia, China, and even against Europe and individual countries within Europe. In many cases, the EU itself imposes sanctions under

Originally, Europe was founded as a peace project that wanted to serve as a model for the world with her innovate model of a voluntary union of states. The early slogan with which the EU offered her model worldwide was "partnership". This policy is seemingly to be continued to this day with the "Partnership and Cooperation Agreements" (PCA), which are offered and negotiated worldwide.[157]

---

pressure from the US, even if they violate its own interests. Euphemistically, this is called "economic war". Not infrequently, however, these sanctions also have deadly consequences, as in the case of countries into which war has been brought, such as Syria, where a population in war is additionally punished with sanctions because the "regime" is not acceptable to the USA and Europe.

[157] The author of this essay has been involved in the implementation of these partnership agreements and association agreements for several decades as an advisor to the EU and various partner countries in several regions of the world. He has therefore had the opportunity to help shape these negotiations and the reform processes since the presidency of Delors. The author has thus seen these political processes from both sides and has played a supporting role in them. It was always important to him to represent the "Europe of Partnership". The Europe of power in the sense of US hegemony was never his intention.

As recent events in Ukraine, but also in North African states such as Egypt, Lebanon, Libya and Syria, as well as in Turkey, show, this instrument of "partnership agreements" is increasingly being used by the EU as an instrument of power to "get states on track" or to keep them in line. Based on this experience of the partner countries, the EU is increasingly perceived worldwide as a growing political power that aims at political and economic "dominance", and is largely subordinate to the goals of the USA as a global hegemonic power.

Since the wars against Yugoslavia and Libya, this image of the EU partnership has experienced very clear cracks in the eyes of many partner countries. In addition, there are the current wars in Syria[158], Iraq,

---

[158] In Syria as in Iraq, American forces are still under "occupation" against the will of the respective governments of these countries. Syria is also suffering unspeakably from the sanctions regime of the USA and the EU.
See also "Syria Crisis and EU: Catastrophic Poverty and Emigration as a Last Resort", 22 February 2024 Thomas Pany. The same applies to "Syria – The Never-Ending (Lying) Story", 20 February 2020, by Tobias Riegel.

Afghanistan and Yemen, all within a few hours' flight of Europe's capitals, in which NATO and some of its important European members are directly involved and actively engaged with armed forces.[159]

In addition to the constantly expanding "peace missions" in North, West and Central Africa, new areas of operation and 'peace missions" in Asia and on all the world's oceans are being considered, and partially being already implemented. We can assume that these ambitions will be perceived both in Latin America, where they currently affect countries such as Bolivia, Chile, Ecuador, Colombia, Peru and Venezuela, as well as in Asia, where, in addition to the nuclear powers China, India and Pakistan, the large countries and important states such as Indonesia, Malaysia and the

---

[159] To illustrate the role that Germany is taking on in Syria and as a member of NATO, here are just two examples: one is the "Germany finances Erdoğan's resettlement policy in northern and eastern Syria, from January 24, 2020, by Elke Dangeleit, and the other one is "Turkey: Merkel's breaking of civilizational taboos", from January 25, 2020, b Tomasz Konicz; both articles have been published in the online magazine Telepolis.

Philippines are keeping a very close eye on the EU's policy of interests and political ambitions. "Big politics" want to present it to us as a sign of strength and sovereignty when France and Germany, in alliance with other European states such as Spain and Italy, join forces to form and build a large and comprehensive industrial-military complex in Europe following the role model of the USA.[160] In their external view, the affected countries from the "Global South" tend to view these clear military ambitions of the EU with suspicion.

Aren't these global events of geopolitical initiatives and activities symptoms of a change of direction, a serious change and massive expansion of the mandates of the EU and NATO? If we have this fear, then we should also ask ourselves whether this is what we want in Europe, and whether, and if so, how, we can determine these geopolitical processes and initiatives

---

[160] Refer to Peter Carstens in the FAZ of January 21, 2020, "German-French Project" - A Fighter Aircraft for 100 Billion Euros".

ourselves as sovereign shapers of our political destiny in Europe.

However, the indications point quite clearly to the fact that we in Europe find ourselves in a contemporary political current, in which we are no longer able to control ourselves to an ever greater extent.

Nowadays, European rearmament and the further expansion and development of a European military-industrial complex are celebrated in grand attire.[161] It is deliberately overlooked that the industrial-military complex in Germany, as well as the entire rest of its economic capacities, are already largely controlled by the American-dominated financial corporations and their

---

[161] As one of many other examples, the article in the

FAZ of 21.01.2020, "German-French project" - A fighter aircraft for 100 billion Euros, should be mentioned here. This rearmament and its public celebration also affects all other branches of arms, such as the establishment of a joint fleet for use on the world's oceans, but especially in Asia directed against China.

instruments.[162] As a consequence, this means that we are witnessing the expansion of the American industrial-military complex on the territory of the EU and are enthusiastically celebrating these events, as if they are in our own interest.[163]

In this sense, we saw in this enthusiasm of the FAZ, Germany's only internationally renowned liberal-conservative daily newspaper, when on July 14, 2019, it "saw the Franco-German brothers marching under arms on the Elysian fields", the symptom of an emerging crisis that we would better have avoided. Unfortunately, this crisis has become real since the war of 2022, has deepened massively and, it is unfortunately to be assumed, has also poured into formal institutional structures

---

[162] As one of the more recent sources, we cite Jens Berger, Who protects the world from the financial corporations?", Frankfurt, 2020.

[163] Very informative is the article by Werner Rügemer in the online magazine "Nachdenkseiten" of April 23, 2019, "USA in decline? – But in the EU, it is more powerful than ever before". By the same author, "The Capitalists of the 21st Century. Generally understandable notes on the rise of the new financial players", Cologne, 2018.

and informal power relations among the EU and NATO.

This title and the picture in the FAZ take up the situation in Europe before the First World War, at least through the spirit, if not with words. In 1914, the French and the Germans were equally enthusiastic, and in the war that followed, they paid dearly, with enormous human sacrifices on both sides. Another war followed, less violent for France, because German troops lec war mainly to Eastern Europe and against Russia, in search of "living space", for raw materials and natural resources, as is the case again in the 21st century.

After this Second World War, France had finally become a member of the United Nations Security Council as one of the winners and had equipped itself with its own arsenal of nuclear weapons.

Politically, Mitterrand was indeed the last Gaullist who wanted to defend the interests of France and Europe in the face of American power. France was the last bastion of conscious resistance against the

Americanization of Europe[164] and against the forced adoption of the one-sided, scientific-technically limited concept of progress of the USA, as well as its hegemonic political claims in Europe and also beyond, on a global level. Since then, France and Europe have gradually withdrawn from this position of resistance to cultural, economic and political appropriation, and have in fact begun to transform their national and European identities in favor of gradual incorporation into the American hegemonic empire.

This is consistently demonstrated by the fact that France has become a full member of NATO again since 2009, and also by the fact that US capital currently controls 50% and more of the assets in Germany and other European countries.[165]

---

[164] On this topic, we refer to the article on "Americanization and Westernization", by Anselm Doering-Manteuffel, in: Docupedia-Zeitgeschichte, 18.1.2011.

[165] As one of many possible sources, we refer to Werner Rügemer, "Die Kapitalisten des 21. Jahrhunderts, Gemeinverständlicher Abriss zum Aufstieg der neuen Finanzakteure", Cologne, 2018.

So, if we look back at the current situation and the joint parade of the French and German armed forces on the Champs-Élysées in 2019, we should understand that the wars that Europe will fight in the future are the imperialist wars of the United States. France and Germany, and thus Europe, have become direct and unconditional allies and vassals of the political, military-industrial and financial hegemonic forces of the United States.

The submission to the interests of the USA and the dissolution of Europe's sovereignty seems to have been decided for the time being and will only be corrected in the foreseeable future by drastic measures and a geopolitical realignment of European foreign policy. Membership in NATO is the critical factor and plays the paramount role here. The uncritical integration of NATO's policy into the geopolitics of the EU has meant the end of the sovereign creative power of its foreign policy. This has also led to Europe turning from a peace project into a global warmonger that is currently waging a proxy war against Russia for the very interests of the USA and within the framework of NATO. For possible corrections in relations with the USA, assessment of Europe's membership in NATO must therefore be the first step to take. As a starting point for the establishment of political relations among sovereign partners, Europe will have to return to the positions of Charles de Gaulle.

FATAL CONSEQUENCES OF THE EU'S ORIENTATION TOWARDS THE WEST: THE AMERICAN "CORDON SANITAIRE" FROM THE BALTIC TO THE BLACK SEA

Since the Maastricht Treaty of 1993, and accelerated after the financial and debt crisis after 2007/08, France has thus succeeded, first, in successfully gaining access to German financial and economic resources through European integration, and then gradually expanding[166] the transfer

---

[166] To understand this rapid development of financial instruments, a glance at the official website of the EU is enough. The sovereignty of the member states is no longer given and depends on the "purse" of the EU: https://www.Europarl.Europa.eu/factsheets/de/sheet/9 1/finanzielle-unterstutzung-der-eu-mitgliedstaaten

of the German resources through the EU's various financial "crisis instruments". Since that time, Germany has willingly submitted to the policies of the EU and the ECB, which has used the common European resources to buy up ultimately uncovered government bonds of the countries from the south of the EU. Likewise, the ECB's mechanisms are accumulating huge Target balances to secure economic liquidity in the southern European member states.[167] In addition, the European Stabilization Mechanism (ESM) was created without setting a limit for it or establishing rules for consistently holding the benefiting countries accountable.[168] Likewise, the banking union will lead to the general liability of the member states among themselves, with the more

---

[167] Prof. Hans-Werner Sinn has critically analyzed the mechanisms of these transfers of German assets to the Southern European countries. Various reports are on his website: https://www.hanswernersinn.de/de
Dr. Daniel Stelter is following in these footsteps: https://think-beyondtheobvious.com/

[168] These developments in the financial and economic sectors of the EU have been most consistently critically followed by Prof. Hans-Werner Sinn: https://www.hanswernersinn.de/de.

"generous" paying the bills for those, who prefer to keep their assets at home. The EU, as a platform for the transfer of virtually all financial and economic resources and unlimited mutual liability for all obligations, has become a reality. Germany has ceded the power to dispose of its assets and all its economic resources to the EU.[169] This picture also fits in with the fact that, according to the latest reports, Germany wants to cede command of its army to NATO, and that means to the USA. This was announced by the German Minister of Defense in his speech on May 10, 2024, at *Johns Hopkins University's School of Advanced International Studies*.

---

[169] Prof. Dieter Spethmann commented on this relatively early when he publicly and empathically warned that "Germany is giving away its prosperity", on January 19, 2011, in the FAZ.

Nowadays, Prof. Sinn, former director of the IFO-Institute in Munich, is probably the most prominent voice to speak out very clearly in public.

But also in the FAZ, the then co-publisher Volker Stelzner, as well as Thomas Mayer, former chief economist of Deutsche Bank, warned urgently against these results for many years.

The particularly fatal issue about this situation is, however, that the United States has become the big winner through the European "communitarization" of German and European resources, in general. Due to the strong dominance of the US financial sector over German industry and the entire German economy[170], which also includes a large part of the banks, as well as the German real estate industry, and since 2022, the entire energy sector as well, this dominance is also being transferred to the entire European economy. Thus, the French-German-British-Spanish industrial-military complex finally becomes an American-dominated enterprise of gigantic proportions, and this on European territory and with European engineering. If we

---

[170] Economic analyses for countries such as Greece, Spain or Italy would certainly confirm these statements. In the years following the Lehman crisis, this trend has intensified, as US-dominated financial instruments have used this period of European weakness to buy up *available* European assets, primarily industrial companies, banks and service providers, cheaply.

assume [171]that, as things stand today, about 50% of the world's arms production[172] comes from the United States, then we will understand that the military dominance of the United States and NATO will be considerably increased by direct access to European industry in this area.

In our understanding, this massive rearmament is not a good sign, because weapons are not primarily built for deterrence, but their primary purpose is to be used in wars, even if it is in so-called "defensive wars".

Yet another fatal result has come to light through the concentration of European integration on the two states of France and Germany. Geographically and geopolitically, Germany has moved out of the center of Europe with this policy. By orienting itself almost exclusively to the West, towards the US and France, Germany has, figuratively speaking, now extended to the Atlantic,

---

[171] We refer here mainly to publicly available figures, such as those from SIPRI.

[172] All information can be found on the website of SIPRI – Stockholm International Peace Research Institute. https://www.sipri.org/databases/armstransfers.

becoming an integral part of the EU under French dominance and within the framework of US hegemony.

At the same time, this has led to the Central and Eastern European states being severely neglected by EU politics for several decades. Even smaller initiatives such as the "Weimar Triangle" with Germany, France and Poland cannot hide this. No one will deny that it has become a German reflex to seek the French partner first and usually exclusively for every problem and challenge in the EU. On the other hand, the German policy of reconciliation, which had been initiated in an impressive way under Willy Brandt, was never understood by Germany in its essence and significance. It is regrettable to see how, since the new open war against Russia, the policy of détente[173], led by politicians such as Willy Brandt, Egon Bahr and Hans-Dietrich Genscher, has been ideologically ostracized in Germany since 2022.

---

[173] See Willy Brandt's biography "Securing Peace and Overcoming Walls – Ost- und Deutschlandpolitik 1955–1989". https://www.willy-brandt-biografie.de/politik/ost-und-deutschlandpolitik/

The consequences of this revisionist and one-sided orientation of German European foreign policy are fatal. In the course of the first decades of the 21st century, the USA succeeded in forming a "cordon sanitaire", i.e. a "buffer zone" in the eastern rear of Germany and the EU within the framework of NATO, successively and strategically very clearly aligned and consistently implemented.[174] The Baltic States, together with Poland, Kosovo, Bulgaria and Romania,[175] have been contractually bound by the USA and NATO and supported militarily with equipment, and today they willingly form the new frontline states of

---

[174] We do not think it is a good sign that US policy today is once again resorting to a concept that was first an instrument of European policy in the period before the First World War. It seems to us like an indication that Europe cannot break away from its past. If we were to fall back into the European politics of wars, which have shaped the continent for many centuries, then that would be fatal.

[175] Since 2014 at the latest, Ukraine has also been included here. Ukraine is neither in the EU nor in NATO, but it has been built up by the US and Great Britain to become the new frontline state against Russia.

NATO and the US hegemonic policy directed against Russia.

For Germany and France, and with them the EU, this means once again being faced with a *fait accompli* and having to accept a policy on the European continent that they themselves have not shaped as sovereign nations. As we have had to learn since 2022, to our deep chagrin, the ground has been prepared for the next big war on the territory of Europe. From the point of view of the United States, the priority objective of its hegemonic policy must be to gain free access to the resources that lie on Russian territory. From the U.S.'s point of view, this is the decisive means of effectively curbing the growth of the Chinese economy and the expansion of China's geopolitical importance and power for all time to come.[176]

---

[176] In the Pacific region, the US is pursuing its ASEAN policy, which has been actively and skillfully pursued since Clinton's first term in office, with the goal of integrating as many Asian countries as possible economically and militarily in order to bring them into vassal status, as the US has successfully succeeded in doing with the European states.

Europe has given up her sovereignty

The EU and practically all European countries have thus definitely given up their sovereignty and independence since the 21st century.

Whether Europe can and wants to regain her sovereignty cannot be answered conclusively. In this analytical study, we saw it as our task to sketch out this process, through which France, Germany and finally the whole of Europe lost the power to shape their policies. Such clarification is required, because only when this awareness has clearly come to light in Europe, will people be able to ask themselves whether they can and want to change the given situation. In any case, it seems that the developments of the past decades have unhinged the basic rules for a functioning democracy in Europe. Because if the people in their countries can no longer decide for themselves about state action, but if, on the contrary, important decisions are made by external institutions and foreign states according to foreign interests, then there can no longer be any talk of democracy. Even the concepts of "multi-level governance", which are very popular in the EU, cannot help to overcome this.[177] Obviously, the level, on which decisions on the destiny of Europe are not taken in Paris or Berlin, neither in Brussels.

The aim of this chapter has been to show the profound transformation that has taken place in Europe since the end of the Second World War. Only through an understanding of the deeper causes, the interdependencies of the actors, and the historical background will it be possible for us to find orientation, bringing us to a situation where we can take up the challenges of the future. Only by overcoming the challenges and the deep and persistent crisis, in which Europe currently finds herself, can new forces

---

[177] There is extensive literature, discussions and one could almost say a "European movement" on "multi-level governance". We just want to note here that, in our view, this prominent concept is diametrically opposed to the claims of "democracy". The concept of "multi-level governance" is therefore ultimately undemocratic and anti-federalist.
The structures of an ESM correspond exactly to this concept. It is explicitly stated in the statutes that responsibility of the acting persons is to be excluded in any case.
In our understanding, however, democracy and responsibility belong inseparably together.

emerge in order to open up new paths and opportunities for the sovereign, peaceful and sustainable design of our living environments and the shaping of our societies.

Guai - The Breakthrough (the Determination)

The best way to fight evil is to make vigorous progress toward the good.

I Ging, das Buch der Wandlungen, in der Übersetzung von Richard Wilhelm

Epilogue – Final Considerations

We do certainly not pretend to present ourselves here as the great specialists of the EU integration process, the policy of NATO enlargement, or even of American foreign policy. For all these fields and areas, there are specialists, who are far superior to us in knowledge and insight.

However, we are convinced that it is our strength to see, understand and also present things, procedures and processes in a broader context, taking a wider view of the complex interdependency of issues and events. In addition, one of our advantages is that we are not dependent on any institution, we are not paid by anyone for our work. In this sense, we owe nothing to anyone, only to our own conscience.

For a critical view of the integration process of the EU, we recommend the work of Ulrike Guérot, who has since been dismissed as a professor from the University of Bonn, ostensibly because of plagiarism accusations, but in fact because she does not want to obey the currently practiced attitude of mainstream politics of the European governments. She had a high price to pay for her honest and sincere efforts to promote European integration. On American foreign policy, we have repeatedly sought information from Henry Kissinger, as an elder statesman and knowledgeable insider. The best source on American foreign policy is certainly the publications of the Council on Foreign Relations (CFR), where one can find all the information required to understand the development of US foreign policy positions over the past century, albeit from a sole American perspective. For a critical observer of current developments in US foreign policy, excellent analyses can be found daily on

Global Times China and are sufficient for a first insight. On the issue of NATO enlargement and extension towards the Russian border, many discussion papers and studies with different points of view are being published; we do not want to highlight one individual source here.

As an attentive observer of current political and social processes, and as a trained economist, political scientist and social anthropologist, I personally have all the prerequisites and analytical skills to arrive at a good understanding of the international relations. In addition, I have worked a lot for the EU over several decades, but also for other international organizations such as the World Bank, the UNDP (*United Nations Development Program*), and the African and Asian Development Banks. So, I also know these institutions from the inside, I know to some extent how they are organized and according to which rules they function. The German and Swiss governments were also among my customers. In my forty-year career, I have provided consulting and advisory services in more than fifty countries on four continents, mostly for governments and their institutions, but also for private companies and banks. I know much of what is talked about in the book from my own experience. I have always learned a lot in my work as an advisor, talking to many people in a great variety of countries, who look at Europe from the outside, or who have looked at Europe from the outside, such as Poland, the Czech Republic or Hungary, when they were not yet members of NATO, i.e. before 1999, and when they were not yet members of the EU, in the years after 1990 to 2003.

So I take the right to make clear statements, because I assume that I have a sufficiently good understanding of the history, the background and the relationships and interdependencies, about which I have written in this book. I have the academic training that qualifies me for this work. In addition, I have sought out many written sources and carefully analyzed them. In my professional career, from 1982 to 2024, I have gained intensive practical experience in coping with a large number of diverse tasks in the context of reform processes in many, often very diverse countries. These statements are made here with the purpose of providing some authority on the analysis presented in this book and on the argumentation and narrative followed by the author.

We have made it clear by now that with this book, we are primarily pursuing the goal of providing information to the European public, opening their eyes about their own situation, as well as for their responsibility. We do not know who will read the book, how it will be understood and received, and what impact it will have. But we know that it will not only be read in Europe. Earlier publications of related subjects and of similar argumentation have in any case met great interest abroad, especially in China and Russia.

Our goal was to present a book that is easy to read and whose argumentation is clear and concise, even if the content and subject matters are often quite complex. The most important message is that Europe has gotten into an existential crisis through its own fault. We believe that Europe must pull herself by her own forces out of the quagmire, into which it has ever deeper fallen over a period of more than a hundred years, as a result of its own failures and deficiencies.

We also wanted to indicate that in such a difficult situation, it is important and can be decisive to understand, who the friends and who the enemies are. Support for one's own efforts should not be rejected, if it helps to find one's way out of the existing difficulties. Due to the internal discord that was common in Europe for a long time, it has been easy for other, ambitious nations, such as the USA, to interfere in the internal shaping of Europe. For centuries, the large countries and states in Europe have repeatedly quarreled through wars and have thus allowed themselves to be brought into ever new and ever greater dependencies. There is still a lack of a healthy self-image of Europe as a common cultural space with shared interests. The egoism of the nation-states is still prevalent and more important than the formulation of common goals and intentions. A brief overview of various EU agendas that have been declared but have never been seriously addressed or implemented would serve as a striking illustration of this fact.[178] The entire

---

[178] The ambition of the 'Lisbon Agenda' or 'Lisbon strategy' of 2000, has been for the European Union (EU) 'to become the most competitive and dynamic

regulatory framework for politics and economics within the EU and other international organizations must be redesigned according to new rules in the interest of finding a new global balance. At the same time, it is in no way enough for the UN Security Council to be equipped with new members. New platforms with new rules for decision-making must be created. The old hierarchies and mechanisms of control of power and money, according to which the important geopolitical decision-making processes have been managed so far, have long since ceased to be appropriate and are outdated.

Europe must once again have a formative influence on geopolitics, not through weapons, but intelligently and with fresh spirit and courage. Europe must once again determine, for herself, who her friends are and how to deal with them. Europe must gain

---

knowledge-based economy in the world, capable of sustainable economic growth with more and better jobs and greater social cohesion'. Nobody in the EU has ever taken this agenda seriously. Other, and "more important" individual agendas of the different EU member states have taken the fore.

a new self-image, not in the face, or in confrontation with a provoked enemy, as the war initiated against Russia in Ukraine shows. Partnership would, in our eyes, provide a good principle to be taken as a starting point for the formation of a new self-image for the EU. We have noticed this in many countries during the time of our international advisory and consulting services for the EU. When partnership among friends was still in the foreground of EU cooperation, we were met with respect, esteem and goodwill from all sides. Now that the EU's foreign policy has aligned herself with NATO and the USA, the quality of the encounters and meetings with people have completely changed. General mistrust, suspicion and often also cynicism are increasingly dominating relations. Of course, EU leaders have done their best during this period to recruit new officers selected to promote their NATO and US driven policies. The partners had understood that EU policies were not primarily a matter of shaping a common future, but that the EU's selfish economic and political interests had moved to the foreground. EU's partners also understood well, who were the partners in the background, who influenced Europe in determining her interests. Europe was no longer considered a sovereign, but rather a dependent geopolitical player of the United States.

Europe must find its way back to a new, sovereign self-image, both for herself and in the eyes of her partners. Europe's new self-image must be based on the self-confidence that it will be possible to shape our lives on our small continent, merely an appendix on the Eurasian continent, the way people want them to be and according to rules that others do not prescribe for us. We have to look for friends, who support us in our efforts to shape this life creatively, who do not want to dominate us, or who want to dictate to us and impose foreign interests on us. This is not an easy task, and it will be difficult, if we look at the economic dependencies, to which we are currently exposed in Europe. The pressure is already enormous, although we have always been told that we can rely on the support of our friends in any situation. If we consider the price we are currently paying for our "friendship" with the US and NATO, then this claim must be questioned, or even directly doubted, and finally rejected as false. Why?

Because the price of this friendship has been enmity toward former friends and partners. The US and NATO have forced us into a block that prohibits us from choosing our partners and friends freely and according to our very own interests. We have all become increasingly aware that we are externally determined and have long since ceased to be able to decide in sovereignty over our own fate.

We assume that people in Europe can find out very well in open discourses what they estimate is important and precious to them, and what is in their interest. For this they do not need foreign masters or self-proclaimed leaders of the power elites. However, to take our chance and come back to a mode, where we take our own sovereign decision again, we have to say goodbye to crisis mode in order to escape the massive pressure created by uncontrolled fear. This is also a fear of taking responsibility and being in charge of our own lives and destiny in Europe. We have to refuse action, which leads us further and further into ever more difficult entanglements and wants us to assume responsibilities that are not our own and do not serve our long-term interests.

The cultural variety of European models of life, which still exist, and we still have the pleasure to enjoy in the countries of Europe, are all under the pressure of uniformity through ever new coercion and through ever stronger influence towards a cultural uniformity. The obstruction and suppression of cultural and intellectual diversity are taking on ever greater dimensions of threat. EU regulations, often under pressure from the US, are increasingly squeezing our cultural diversity and enclosing individual and creative European communication patterns into narrow-minded and one-dimensional limits. This has already become evident, in particular at the time of the Corona policy, when we were all forced to follow rules that we did not know, where they came from, or who had set them up[179]. An epidemic, a so-called pandemic, was conjured up, of which there were no symptoms, except for the fear that has been planted in the citizens of Europe by so-called global power elites[180].

---

[179] Refer to Rand Paul's "Deception: The Great Covid Cover-Up", published on October 10, 2023.
[180] It is official now that Anthony Fauci, in charge of Corona policies under President Trump, has been lying

These processes of public manipulation have taken on increasingly threatening forms since the German and European public have been called upon and often forced to demonize Russia and turn culturally against China[181]. These are extremist attitudes and authoritarian political processes that cannot be accepted in any way in open and free societies. They all represent attitudes and rules of action that cannot find any justification in reality, but are imposed on us by power elites who think they do not have to justify themselves for them. The international community was given rules of action by individual "Western" nations and "Western"-dominated institutions, such as WHO, that could no longer be questioned. These events are examples of how the future system of global governance must not be regulated, if it is to enable an improved quality of life for all

---

not only about the origin of the Coronavirus, but has also suggested protective measures that have been an outgrow of his private, single-minded intentions. Refer to: InfoSperber, 23.02.2024; refer to:
https://www.infosperber.ch/gesundheit/anthony-fauci-hat-ueber-das-corona-virus-gelogen/

[181] Think of the suppression of Confucian institutes and other cultural initiatives in Germany and Europe.

and the development of more freedom, as well as the chance for peaceful and prosperous coexistence for all nations and peoples.

This book therefore wants to serve to raise awareness, which is the most important prerequisite on the path to creating a new European self-confident self-image. In the Analytical Psychology of C.G. Jung, this is called "the individuation process", i.e. knowing progressively and with increasing self-trust, who you are.

EUROPE'S STEP OUT OF THE CRISIS

We see Europe in an extremely difficult situation today. It will be very difficult for Europe to find its way out of these difficulties on its own. In freeing itself from this "political and economic trap" into which Europe has fallen, it will be very helpful to find the support of friends and partners. Europe will have to look for new friends, or revive proven partnerships. In order to form new partnerships, Europe will have to set her own goals, because the friends will want to know where the journey together is going to be headed.

The paradigm shift that Europe will have to undergo will require Europe to give herself the opportunity to reposition herself geopolitically. To do this, Europe must develop its own sovereign profile. Europe must redefine her role in the emerging multipolar world. This also means that Europe should not integrate herself into new alliances for the time being. Joining other alliances presupposes a healthy and self-confident self-image, which must first be developed again in Europe.

After the collapse of the Soviet Union and German reunification, the window for such a new role for Europe was open for a short time. However, it seems that Europe and the EU have not been ready at that time. The EU has been occupied by other important processes and has not yet consolidated her internal structures[182]. After the attack on the World Trade Center in 2001, the US

---

[182] Remember that these have been the internal processes leading to the Maastricht Treaty under EU President Delors, and the subsequent introduction of the Euro currency.

intensified its foreign policy with the aim of achieving and consolidating its hegemonic dominance[183]. The United States was the only superpower to emerge from the Cold War. The time had come to consolidate this hegemonic position. Europe and the EU have been considered the main partners in the implementation of the American strategy of geopolitical hegemony. Europe went with the USA to Iraq, Afghanistan, and EU Member States also took over the task of bombing Libya on behalf of the USA. The reception of Syrian refugees and the deal with Turkey to manage the flow of refugees are also part of this period. Europe had fallen straight into the American fairway, without the possibility of determining its own fate. Of course, this has also affected relations with Europe's existing partners. Europe's international relations have been massively damaged, especially by the increasingly aggressive sanctions policy and the US' nationalist economic policy, in the years since the war in Ukraine. Russia has,

---

[183] A very informative source of information is Gore Vidal, with several fascinating and elucidating books. One striking example is Gore Vidal's "Perpetual War for Perpetual Peace: How we got to be so hated. American Imperialism, Book 1", 2002.

intentionally and with strong support from managed media, mutated into an enemy, to whom war has been declared. China has become a major adversary, because it does not want to subordinate itself to American interests. Europe has been forced to join these American political positions unconditionally. As a result, the geopolitical image of Europe has suffered great damage. This also applies to individual countries in Europe. The diplomatic damage from following American policy and the expansive NATO strategy is huge. As an author, I can confirm this from my own professional experience in the international political arena, without reservation.

In such a situation, as we briefly outline it here, the well-known saying fits very well: "If you have such friends, you don't have to worry about enemies". This is especially true for NATO. If Europe wants to play its own, independent and sovereign role, as a global partner in the future, then it must detach itself from NATO and gradually withdraw.[184]

---

[184] It is astonishing to see how the small and not very rich country of Hungary, as a member of the EU and NATO, does not want to subordinate itself to the

This also means that previous friendships no longer have to remain valid unconditionally and in their existing form. It also means that previous enmities can be ended. New relationships will have to be established to replace old ones in a steady process. Europe does not need this NATO for its prosperous and peaceful development. Europe is not threatened, neither by Russia nor by China, and not even by the USA. NATO has mutated into an instrument that primarily does not serve Europe's security, but is subordinated to the geopolitical interests of the United States and its hegemonic aspirations. The decoupling of Europe from NATO will therefore be the first and decisive step toward a paradigm shift in Europe, as a prerequisite for Europe to play a new,

---

constraints of these institutions without resistance. In a news item in the Hungarian online magazine *Hungary Today* on May 24, 2024, we read that Hungary refuses to participate directly in the war against Russia. Hungary puts forward a very intelligent argument, insisting that NATO stands for itself as a "defensive alliance". Therefore, members cannot be forced into wars of aggression. This shows that alternatives to unconditional submission to the dictates of the USA and NATO are possible.

sovereign geopolitical role in the future. If Europe leaves NATO, or at least the major European nations, such as France, Germany, Italy, the Netherlands and Spain, will take this decision, then the paradigm shift will have been set into motion. Therefore, this is the first and decisive step to breaking free from the clutches of the USA. The priorities in economic cooperation will then also have to be redefined. Due to the intense economic integration between the US and Europe, this will take time. But the dominance and almost exclusive economic fixation on the USA will have to be gradually scaled back, to the advantage of intensifying economic relations with other countries, above all with China, India and Russia. Europe must create a new balance between the old and large partner, the USA, and the new partners from Asia, Eurasia, Latin America and Africa.

The crisis for Europe is here. It can no longer be denied. Two possibilities are open, two paths, of which only the second will be a successful way out of the crisis. Either Europe can continue as before, and submit to the hegemonic striving of the USA driven by NATO, i.e. ultimately without the direct responsibility of the nation-states. Europe will then become part of a new world order, but as an integrated part of a Western, US-dominated bloc, without the possibility of playing an independent and sovereign role. This way, Europe will always remain a junior partner of the United States, to whose bloc it will belong.

In an alternative scenario, Europe can work her way out of the crisis on its own, remembering her own interests, setting her own sovereign goals again, and developing her own strategy and road map.

EUROPE'S NEW SELF-IMAGE, GROWN OUT OF HER HISTORY AND CULTURE

At this stage we will briefly recall the purpose of this book and explain our motivation for writing it. The primary interest does not consist of pointing out the problems. Rather, we intend to show ways that can lead to feasible solutions for problems and existing challenges. The working of the intellect requires, however, that we first start with an analysis of the situational context and its historical background. Therefore, we started the book with the Treaty of Versailles and its consequences for Europe under US leadership. At this very moment in history, the seeds have been planted, of which our current problems have grown out. In the next step, we provided details on the creation of the EU and her administrative and political structures, showing closely the influence the US has taken on these processes and how this informed the specific organizational structure of the EU. With our analytical approach, we intended to identify the root causes of the current problems and challenges Europe and the world are facing. Only through the knowledge of the root causes and their impact can appropriate measures be identified that will lead to sustainable solutions for existing problems. To spell it out clearly: This book has been drafted in a creative process, without fixed ideas at the outset, a process, in which the outcome has not been known at the outset. Through an intellectual and analytical process, a deep understanding of the current situation has been created. We are convinced that only on the basis of such an honestly led scientific and intellectual endeavor can thorough understanding be achieved and meaningful orientation for future action be provided. Our endeavor has focused on Europe and the new system of global governance. We see ourselves now, reaching the end of our intellectual and analytical process, in a position to make confident and convincing suggestions for measures to be taken. You may call this intellectual and analytical process a method to find truths for access to understanding reality. It is our personal conviction that only such an honest and transparent process can lead to results that may convince other people of their value as an orientation for future action.

We have shown how Europe got into this crisis and are now in a position to point to concrete measures for Europe to find her way out of the crisis. On the basis of our honest and transparent analysis, we are now in a position to provide orientation for action, which our political leaders and self-declared figures of our present power elites have, blinded or intentionally, not given. Europe is in today's crisis, because it has not had the will to take its fate into its own hands for more than a century. Until the First World War, only individual states and monarchic empires had taken responsibility for themselves and for the pursuit of their specific interests. Europe was divided, and the nations repeatedly fought each other in fierce wars. The 'Hundred Years War' between England and France and the Napoleonic Wars can serve as striking examples from pre-modern times. The Habsburg Empire also owed its expansion and dimension either to wars of aggression in Italy, in Central Europe, on the Balkans, or still in defensive wars against the Turks. In the 20th century, these wars reached their inglorious climax with the two Europe-driven world wars. Europe emerged weakened in 1919, and even more so in 1945, while the USA was able to present itself as the new global empire that emerged to become the new globally dominant power. It is therefore not far from the truth to say that the European powers have gotten into their current crisis through their own failure, which has come to a head in our time. With these considerations alone, we show that we are fundamentally in favor of the EU and European integration and want to continue to promote them. However, the Europe must free itself from the clutches of NATO, eventually finding and redefining her own way, leading to a coexistence in Europe that is shaped according to her own rules.

If we want to gain a still deeper understanding of the situation in Europe, we must also ask ourselves, why this crisis is currently coming to a head and what the concrete reasons for the culmination of the situation are. Again, the answer is not difficult to find, if we dare to be honest. Europe's crisis is coming to a head, because the United States has increasingly fallen into a crisis that arises, on the one hand, from internal contradictions that increasingly call into question the financial viability of its own hegemonic and military ambitions. In addition, the crisis of American hegemony also has to do with the growing countervailing forces of other nations and alliances. However, the United States does not accept to retreat from its hegemonic strive, it does not modify and adapt its previous line and strategy. The US is prepared to use any means to avoid losing its dominance in this crisis, and is taking up any challenge to even emerge stronger from it. Due to the almost absolute subordination of

Europe, within the framework of NATO, to the strategic aspirations of the USA, the crisis of the USA has today become the crisis of Europe.

If we look at the situation this way, then it also becomes clear how the way out of the crisis can be found. Europe does not have to decouple herself from the USA, that will not be possible and is ultimately not even desirable. The United States will always remain a privileged partner of Europe and within her international relations network. However, the US cannot remain the dominant or the single most important partner of Europe. Obviously, Europe must resist the hegemonic ambitions of the USA. Europe must not allow herself to be made a henchman for the wars of the USA, which are now being waged worldwide via NATO's military platform and continue to be propagated and prepared continuously.[185]

---

[185] In line with our argumentation, Sevim Dağdelen, Member of the Bundestag and specialist for the Middle East, has recently published a comprehensive book "NATO: A Reckoning with the Alliance of Values", 2024.

In line with our argument in this book, we must also point out, in all honesty, that the evil of the belief in unlimited growth in all areas and at all levels has its roots in Europe. This is where the modern sciences originated. Until the 1920s, practically all Nobel Prize winners in the natural sciences were educated in Europe and had reached their impact on European development[186]. All the knowledge needed for the formation of modern sciences comes from Europe. Oppenheimer, who led the team to build the first atomic bomb, was trained by Max Planck in Göttingen and Niels Bohr in Copenhagen. This European origin and the development of the foundations of modern science up to the Second World War apply to everything from mathematics to chemistry, physics and astrophysics.

In the period after the Second World War, i.e. after 1945, the USA perfected European science and, in particular, continued the technological application of the results of the

---

[186] Modris Eksteins also points out the link between science and cultural development in his historic novel, "Rites of Spring: The Great War and the Birth of the Modern Age", published in 2000.

sciences intensively and pragmatically[187]. Not only did all the knowledge required to build the atomic bomb come from Europe to the USA, but also the knowledge in the other sciences. A striking example is provided by the work of Norbert Wiener[188] and John von Neumann, both former members of the Vienna Circle, who jointly created the science of cybernetics in the US. As an impact of the Second World War and the forced emigration of a great part of the European scientific community, most Nobel Prize winners in the natural and economic sciences have since 1945 come from the USA. But not only the sciences have been perfected in the USA, but also the belief in progress without end and in all areas has been raised to new heights in the USA. As a result, the sciences have

---

[187] Sigmund Freud made an interesting observation about this pragmatism in his lectures on psychoanalysis held in the USA. On the occasion of a lecture, he says that he did not dare talk about dreams and dream analysis in these lectures, because this must remain incomprehensible to such a "pragmatic people" as the Americans. Everyone knows that dream analysis is at the heart of Freud's psychoanalysis.

[188] Norbert Wiener, "Cybernetics or Control and Communication in the Animal and the Machine", 1948.

increasingly grown into one-sidedness, in which priority is given to the development of technology, in pursuit of the aim to increase the power of humans over nature and to make quick economic profits. It is also well known that the most important technological innovations of the last hundred years have either been developed directly out of the needs of warfare, or have been able to prove their "value" and importance in related processes. Just think of the aircraft industry, or today's drones for military use. If the US were not waging wars directly, then their political and economic driving forces would always consist of their striving for more power and greater wealth. Greater prosperity, for all, was more of a by-product of these efforts. A good example of this approach is offered by John D. Rockefeller, who, as a deeply religious Christian, missed no opportunity to ruthlessly eliminate his competitors, who stood in his way of building up his own business as an Empire, using all the means at his disposal. The aggressiveness that characterized him, together with his irrepressible drive for business success, was the key to his wealth and power.[189]

We are aware that scientific research and its overwhelming technological effects have resulted in an infinite amount of good and important results for humanity. We can say without hesitation that here in Europe, over the past six hundred years, the modern, individualistic scientist has been formed. All this represents, indisputably, a great step in the development of humanity. The dilemma that Europe has found itself in at the same time, however, has its origin in the fact that Europe has not yet found a counterweight to this one-sided scientific and technological development, helping her to achieve a balance[190]. Social and political developments in Europe have not kept pace with this scientific and technological progress. The

---

[189] This contradictory personality is very convincingly shown in Robert Greene's book "The Laws of Human Nature", of 2019, in the chapter on "aggressiveness". The English original is "The Laws of Human Nature, 2018.

[190] The attentive reader will not overlook that, with our indication of the lack of balance, we are hinting at the need for the spiritual balancing powers between East and West.

formation of the EU was certainly an important step in the right direction to free Europe from the old constraints and contradictions on her way to find and follow new rules for her development. This important step also clearly indicates what the decisive challenge is for Europe in our time to actually break the old framework. This challenge is concerning the sovereign restructuring and shaping of our European societies, which must be carried out accordingly by new rules leading to a balance of energies in a self-regulated system of freely uniting European nations and peoples. The time has ripened now for taking up this challenge of establishing new rules rationally and with all the courage required, in order to seize the emerging opportunity to overcome the current crisis. Please remember the famous words: *every crisis offers a chance for new happiness*.

In our understanding, it is useful to recall the important burdens we in Europe have to bear as a result of our history. For the formation of a new self-image of Europe, it is therefore important to understand the great loss Europe has suffered as a result of the

National Socialist ideology. The great loss that Europe has suffered as a result of this National Socialist ideology and its pronounced anti-Semitism after 1920, consists in the emigration of Jewish scientists, the Jewish-European educated middle class, and also important cultural bearers, most of whom emigrated or were fleeing to the USA. Europe has profoundly been impoverished, scientifically and in particular culturally, due to anti-Semitism[191]. Today, we can only understand this retrospectively, and with the help of works such as the autobiography "The World of Yesterday" by Stefan Zweig, who lost his civil existence twice. First, with the collapse of the Habsburg monarchy through the First World War, and then through persecution by the National Socialist regime in Germany, from which he, like thousands of other Jews, could only escape by emigrating. Emigration has brought a large part of the wealth of European science to the USA, while another, perhaps even larger, part has been

---

[191] We recall here the fact that anti-Semitism had become part of the fascist European movement. However, anti-Semitism has been part of the Christian driven ideology of most of European peoples and countries.

silenced in the extermination camps. These events are not only the cause of great shame, but they have also caused enormous damage to Europe, its science, economy and culture.

We should not conceal these roots of today's crisis. It is important for our self-image that we understand the origins of the present European crisis. In this way, we are creating the conditions for taking on responsibility. Responsibility, not necessarily in the moral retrospective sense, but responsibility for creating a better future for all people on our planet. Hence, we call for Europe to take responsibility for its past in order to reformulate its self-image, finding the courage to take responsibility for the future anew.

Bibliography

Abelshauser, Werner; Wunder gibt es immer wieder: Mythos Wirtschaftswunder, in: Aus Politik und Zeitgeschichte, 68 (2018) 27, S. 4-10.

Ansprenger, Franz; Auflösung der Kolonialreiche, 1989.

Armstrong, Karen; The Great Transformation: The Axial Age, 2005. Deutsch: Achsenzeit der grossen Zivilisationen, 2006.

Attali, Jacques; Biographie: C'était François Mitterand, Paris, 2007.

Bateson, Gregory; Geist und Natur. Eine notwendige Einheit, 1987.

Bateson, Gregory; in Ökologie des Geistes, Teil VI, Krisen in der Ökologie des Geistes, von Versailles zur Kybernetik, Vorlesung von 1966.

Bateson, Gregory; Ökologie des Geistes, 1985; English edition: Steps to an Ecology of Mind, Collected Essays, 1972.

Bell, Daniel A, Amitav Acharya, Rajeev Bhargava, Yan Xuetong (eds.); Bridging two Worlds, Comparing Classical Political Thought and Statecraft in India and China, 2003. University of California Press, series: Great Transformations.

Benjamin, Craig G.; Foundations of Eastern Civilization,

Berger, Jens; Wer schützt die Welt vor den Finanzkonzernen?, Frankfurt, 2020.

Bernstein, Richard J.; Beyond objectivism and relativism: Science, Hermeneutics, and Praxis, University of Pennsylvania Press 1983.

Bittner, Wolfgang; Die Eroberung Europas durch die USA, 2015.

Blankart, Charles B.; Föderalismus in Deutschland und in Europa, 2007, erschienen in der Reihe „Neue Studien zur Politischen Ökonomie", Nomos Verlag.

Blankart, Charles B.; Öffentliche Finanzen in der Demokratie: Eine Einführung in die Finanzwissenschaft, Gebundene Ausgabe, 2017.

Bloch, Marc; Die Feudalgesellschaft, Neuausgabe 2019, Französisches Original von 1939.

Bono, Edward de; Lateral Thinking: a Textbook of Creativity, 1970.

Bono, Edward de; Laterales Denken : Ein Kursbuch zur Erschliessung ihrer Kreativitätsreserven, 1971.

Bördlein, Christoph; Einführung in die Verhaltensanalyse (English edition: Introduction to Behavioral Analysis), 2015.

Born, Max; Der Mensch und das Atom, in: Ausblick auf die Zukunft, 1968.

Bozo, Frederic; Deux stratégies pour l'Europe, Paris, 1996.

Bracher, Andreas; Europa im amerikanischen Weltsystem, Bruchstücke zu einer ungeschriebenen Geschichte des 20. Jahrhunderts, 2001.

Bracher, Andreas; Völkische Selbstbestimmung und Dreigliederung, in der Zeitschrift Perseus, der Europäer, Jg. 6 Nr. 8, Juni 2002.

Brandt, Willy; Frieden sichern und Mauern überwinden – Ost- und Deutschlandpolitik 1955–1989. https://www.willy-brandt-biografie.de/politik/ost-und-deutschlandpolitik/

Braudel, Fernand; Die lange Dauer. in: Schriften zur Geschichte, Bd. 1: Gesellschaft und Zeitstrukturen. 1992, S. 49–87. Ganz wichtig in unserem Zusammenhang ist „Die Geschichte der Zivilisation vom 15 bis zum 18 Jahrhundert, 1982.

Braudel, Fernand; Histoire et Sciences sociales : La longue durée, in : Annales, Année 1958, pp. 725-753.

Braudel, Fernand; L'Identité de la France, auf Deutsch herausgegeben als «Frankreich, Band 1: Raum und Geschichte / Band 2: Die Menschen und die Dinge / Band 3: die Dinge und die Menschen, 2009.

Braudel, Fernand; La dynamique du capitalisme. Paris, 1985. Deutsch als: Die Dynamik des Kapitalismus, 1991.

Braun, Eduard; Pseudoliberale Staatsinterventionen und die Neoklassik . Gedanken zum Homo Oeconomicus und zum wahren Wert der Dinge, Mises Institute, Mises Wire, 11. April 2022.

Bricker, Darrell and Ibbitson, John; Empty Planet: The Shock of Global Population Decline, 2019

Briggs, John und Peat, F. David; Die Entdeckung des Chaos, 1997; das Original ist 1989 unter dem Titel „Turbulent Mirror" in New York veröffentlicht worden.

Brzezinski, Zbigniew, The Grand Chessboard: American Primacy and its Geostrategic Imperatives, 1997.

Brzezinski, Zbigniew; Die einzige Weltmacht: Amerikas Strategie der Vorherrschaft, 1999.

Burkhard, Jakob; Kultur der Renaissance in Italien, Erstveröffentlichung 1860.

Butterwegge, Christoph; Die zerrissene Republik. Wirtschaftliche, soziale und politische Ungleichheit in Deutschland, 2019.

Campbell, Joseph; Thou art That. Transforming Religious Metaphor. The spiritual meaning of Biblical Stories, Miracles and Parables, 2002.

Campbell, Joseph; Understanding and Interpretation of Mythology. The Website of the Joseph Campbell Foundation: https://www.jcf.org/.

Fritjof; Tao der Physik, 1977.

Carstens, Peter; Deutsch-Französisches Projekt: Ein Kampfflugzeug für 100 Milliarden Euro, in der FAZ vom 21.01.2020.

Carter, Robert; Frank Lloyd Wright, A Biography, 2006.

Chomsky, Noam; Sprache und Geist, 1970. Darin der Anhang aus *New Left Review* (Nummer 57, September/Oktober 1969).

Chomsky, Noam; Rules and Representations. Behavioral and Brain Sciences, 1980. . Deutsch: Regeln und Repräsentationen, 1980

Chomsky, Noam; Gespräch mit C. J. Polychroniou zum Thema „Warum China, nicht Russland die US-dominierte Weltordnung bedroht", auf Deutsch am 09.07.2022 in Telepolis; Original in Trouthout.

Chomsky, Noam; in Asia-Pacific-Forum vom 31.12.2012, Revenge Of History: Chomsky on Japan, China, The United States, And The Threat of Conflict in Asia".

Clark, Christopher; Die Schlafwandler: Wie Europa in den Ersten Weltkrieg zog, 2013.

Clark, Christopher; Von Zeit und Macht, 2918.

Club of Rome, Grenzen des Wachstums, 1962.

Couvée, Leonard; Verslumung als Folge von Metropolisierung, 2016.

Covey, Stephen R.; Die 7 Wege zur Effektivität, Original von 1990, deutsch 1996.

Dagdelen, Sevim; Die NATO: Eine Abrechnung mit dem Wertebündnis, 2024.

Dangeleit, Elke; Deutschland finanziert Erdogans Umsiedelungspolitik in Nord- und Ostsyrien, Online Magazin Telepolis, vom 24. Januar 2020.

Davis, Irvine Mike; Planet der Slums, Department of History an der University of California, 2005; Planet der Slums ist 2019 auf Deutsch erschienen.

Denson, John V.; "A Century of War" wurde 1997 als Vortrag zum fünfzehnjährigen Jubiläum des Ludwig von Mises Institute gehalten und Mises.org veröffentlicht.

Desjardins, T. ; François Mitterand: un socialiste gaullien, Paris, 1978.

Diamond, Jared; Guns, Germs and Steel. The Fates of Human Societies, 1998.

Doering-Manteuffel, Anselm; Amerikanisierung und Westernisierung, Version: 2.0, in: Docupedia-Zeitgeschichte, 19.08.2019.

Dresdener gesammelte Kommentare zur Sicherheitspolitik – dgksp-diskussionspapiere – vom 14. April 2021.

Duerr, Hans-Peter; Der Mythos vom Zivilisationsprozeß, 2005.

Conze, Eckart; Hegemonie durch Integration: Die amerikanische Europapolitik und ihre Herausforderung durch de Gaulle, in: Institut für Zeitgeschichte, Vierteljahreshefte für Zeitgeschichte, Jahrgang 43 (1995), Heft 2.

Egli, Rene; Das Lola Prinzip, Die Vollkommenheit der Welt, 1994.

Ehrlich, Paul R.; The Population Bomb, New York: Ballantine Books 1968; dt. Übers.: Die Bevölkerungsbombe, 1971.

Eksteins, Modris; Rites of Spring: The Great War and the Birth of the Modern Age, 1989.

Evans, Richard; The Pursuit of Power, Europe 1815-1914, 2016.

Ferguson, Niall; Colossus: The Rise and Fall of the American Empire, 2004.

Ferguson, Niall; Eine Nation ist kein Individuum, und ein Individuum ist keine Nation, am 31.12.2021 in der NZZ.

Ferguson, Niall; Empire: How Britain Made the Modern World, 2003.

Ferguson, Niall; The Ascent of Money: A Financial History of the World, 2008.

Ferguson, Niall; The Cash Nexus. Money and Power in the Modern World, 1700–2000, 2001.

Ferguson, Niall; The War of the World: History's Age of Hatred, 1st Edition, 2009.

Fix, Andrew C.; The Renaissance, the Reformation and the Rise of Nations", Audible Audiobook series: „The Great Courses" produced by „The Teaching Company", 2005.

Focus Magazin Nr. 8, 2009; "Alles schon gelaufen?", Wem gehört Deutschland?

Foreign Affairs, Volume 103 Number 3, No Substitute for Victory, 2024. https://www.foreignaffairs.com/united-states/no-substitute-victory-pottinger-gallagher

Fortes, Meyer; The Political Systems of the Tallensi of the Northern Territories of the Gold Coast, in African Political Systems, M. Fortes and E.E. Evans-Pritchard (eds.), First Edition 1940.

Frankopan, Peter; The Silk Roads, The New History of the World, 2015.

Freud, Sigmund; Vorlesungen zur Einführung in die Psychoanalyse, 1917.

Friedrich, Marc und Weik, Matthias ; Komplette, legale Enteignung per Gesetz, 2019.

Fröhlich, Stefan; Die transatlantischen Beziehungen, Deutschland, 2017.

Fuller, R. Buckminster; Critical Path, 1981;

Fuller, R. Buckminster; Ideas and Integrities, 1963.

Fuller, R. Buckminster; Nine Chains to the Moon", 1938.

Fuller, R. Buckminster; Operating Manual for Spaceship Erath, 1969; deutsche Ausgabe: Bedienungsanleitung für das Raumschiff Erde und andere Schriften", 2011.

Gluckman, Max; The Limits of Naivety in Social Anthropology", 2017.

Goethe, J. W.; Faust, Tragödie Erster und Zweiter Teil, 1986.

Granet, Marcel; Die chinesische Zivilisation. Band 2: Das chinesische Denken. Inhalt, Form, Charakter, Ersterscheinung deutsch 1985. Original: „La pensée chinoise", Paris 1938.

Greene, Robert; Die Gesetze der menschlichen Natur, 2019; das englische Original „The Laws of Human Nature, 2018.

Greene, Robert; Gesetze der Macht. engl. The Laws of Power, 1998.

Grenoble University, Ecole de Management (GEM) de Grenoble, Energie for Society, Université de Grenoble, Politiques énergétiques : comment éviter une dystopie européenne?, 2024.
Griffin, George Edward; The Creature from Jekyll Island, 1994.

Grün, Arno; Dem Leben entfremdet, 2019.

Guelzo, Allen C., et al.; The History of the United States, 2003, 2nd Edition, 2013.

Guilford, J. P.; The Structure of Intellect, in Psychological Bulletin, Volume 53 N° 4, July 1956.

Habermas, Jürgen; Theorie des kommunikativen Handelns, 1981.

Hahn, Robert; Herrschaft von Lissabon bis Wladiwostok", 06.07.2022.

Hayek Friedrich A. v.; Weltwirtschaftliches Archiv, 36. Bd., 1932.

Hayes, Sam W. and Morris, Christopher (eds.): Manifest Destiny and Empire: American Antebellum Expansionism, 1997. Heer, Burkhard; Umwelt, Bevölkerungsdruck und Wirtschaftswachstum in Entwicklungsländern, 2013.

Hegel G.W.F.; Tagebuch der Reise in die Berner Oberalpen, 1796. In: K. Rosenkranz, G.W.F. Hegels Leben [1844]. Darmstadt 1969: 470–89.

Heinsohn, Gunnar; Söhne und Weltmacht, 1. Auflage 2005.

Heisterkamp, Jens (Hg.); Die
Jahrhundertillusion. Wilsons
Selbstbestimmungsrecht der Völker,
Sammelband, 2002.

Hellmann, Gunther; Zwischen
Gestaltungsmacht und Hegemoniefalle: Zur
neuesten Debatte über eine neue deutsche
Außenpolitik, in der Reihe „Aus Politik und
Zeitgeschichte, 11.07.2016.

Heylighen, Francis; , Accelerating Evolution,
2007, in Modelski, Tessaleno and Thompson,
William (eds.), "Globalization as an
Evolutionary Process: Modeling Global
Change", Rethinking Globalizations, London
2007.

Hobsbawm, Eric; Zeitalter der Extreme,
Weltgeschichte des 20. Jahrhunderts, 1995.

Horkheimer, Max und Adorno, Theodor W.;
Dialektik der Aufklärung, 1944.

Horsman, Reginald; Race and Manifest
Destiny: The Origins of American Racial
Anglo-Saxonism, 1981.

Hülsmann, Jörg Guido; Abundance, Generosity, and the State: an Inquiry into Economic Principles, 2024.

Hummel, Diana; Der Bevölkerungsdiskurs: Demographisches Wissen und politische Macht, 2000.

Hungary Today, Online Magazin vom 24. Mai 2024.

Hürter, Thomas; Das Zeitalter der Unschärfe, 2021.

Jordan, Pascual; Wie sieht die Welt von morgen aus?, 1958.

Jung, C. G.; Biographie: Erinnerungen, Träume, Gedanken, 1962.

Jung, C. G.; Modern Men in Search of a Soul", auf Deutsch „Der moderne Mensch auf der Suche nach einer Seele", von 1933.

Keynes, John Maynard; Krieg und Frieden: Die wirtschaftlichen Folgen des Vertrags von Versailles, 1920.

Koestler, Arthur and Smythies, J. R. (eds);
Revolutionizing the Sciences of Man, 1968.

Koestler, Arthur; Jenseits von Atomismus und
Holismus – Der Begriff des Holons, in, "Das
Neue Menschenbild – Die Revolutionierung
der Wissenschaften vom Menschen", 1970,
Hrsg. Arthur Koestler und J. R. Smythies.

Kohlenberg, Kerstin und Schieritz, Mark; am
23. Oktober 2014, in DIE ZEIT Nr. 44/2014,
Die Superwaffe des Mr. Glaser, Sanktionen
gegen Russland und den Iran: Wie
amerikanische Finanzbeamte zu
Wirtschaftskriegern werden.

Konersmann, Ralf (Hrsg.); Kulturkritik:
Reflexionen in der veränderten Welt, Reclam
2001.

Konicz, Tomasz; Türkei: Merkels
zivilisatorischer Tabubruch, Online Magazin
Telepolis, vom 25. Januar 2020.

Koselleck, Reinhard; Vergangene Zukunft.
Zur Semantik geschichtlicher Zeiten, 1989.

Kreitner, R. & Kinicki, A; Organizational Behavior, 2004, New York: McGraw-Hill.

Krohne, Heinz W.; Psychologie der Angst, 2010.

Kuhn, Thomas S.; The Structure of Scientific Revolutions, 1962.

Lau, Jörg; "Regelbasierte Weltordnung. In 80 Phrasen um die Welt", 01. Juli 2020.

Lee, Kuam Yew; From Third World to First, 2016.

Lévi-Strauss, Claude; Das wilde Denken, 1976.

Li Xuanmin and Fan Anqi; Government of China „White paper", in Global Times China, 19. Januar 2023, https://www.globaltimes.cn//author/Reporter -Li-Xuanmin.html.

Lieven, Dominic (ed.); The Cambridge History of Russia, 2005.

Lohmann, Sascha; in SWP-Aktuell 2019/A 31, Mai 2019, Extraterritoriale US-Sanktionen.

Lorenz, Konrad und Wuketits, Franz (Hg.): Die Evolution des Denkens. Zwölf Beiträge, 1983.

Lorenz, Konrad; Das sogenannte Böse: Zur Naturgeschichte der Aggression, 1963.

Lovelock, James; Gaia. A New Look at Life on Earth, 1972.

Lukács, Georg; Die Zerstörung der Vernunft, 1955.

Mackinder, Halford; Artikel „The Geographical Pivot of History, 1904.

Mahlmann, Matthias; Philosophische Grundlehren, 7. Auflage, 2022. https://www.rwi.uzh.ch/elt-lst-mahlmann/rechtstheorie/kant/de/html/unit_u 2.html.

Marschall, Tim; The Future of Gegography, 2023.

Mausfeld, Rainer; Warum schweigen die Lämmer?, 2018.

Mayer, Thomas; Die Ordnung der Freiheit und ihre Feinde: Vom Aufstand der Verlassenen gegen die Herrschaft der Eliten, 2018.

Meadows, H. Donella; Thinking in Systems, 2008.

Mereschkowski, Dmitri; Leonardo da Vinci, 1951.

Merk, Frederick; Manifest Destiny and Mission in American History: A Reinterpretation, 1963.

Mises, Ludwig von; Human Action: A Treatise on Economics, 1949.

Mises, Ludwig von; Theorie des Geldes und der Umlaufmittel, 1912.

Mises, Ludwig von; Vom Wert der besseren Ideen, Vorlesungen, 1958.

Mittasch, Alwin; Von der Chemie zur Philosophie, 1948.

Mohr, Daniel; „Viele amerikanische Investoren, Der Dax ist fest in ausländischer Hand", FAZ vom 26.01.2017.

Morland, Paul; The Power of Demography to Understand Our World, 2019.

Mumford, Lewis; The Original American edition: The Transformation of Man, 1956.

Mumford, Lewis; Mythos der Maschine. Kultur, Technik und Macht, 1986.

Mumford, Lewis; Technics and Civilization, 1934.

Mumford, Lewis; The Condition of Man, 1944.

Mumford, Lewis; The Culture of Cities, 1938.

Mumford, Lewis; The Story of Utopias, 1922.

Needham, Joseph; Moulds of Understanding, 1976.

Needham, Joseph; Needham Research Institute, Science and Civilisation in China, since 1954.

Needham, Joseph; Wissenschaftlicher Universalismus, 1979, das Kapitel „Der Zeitbegriff im Orient", s. 176-250.

Neubauer, Heinz; Grundlagen der Systemtheorie, 1989.

Nietzsche, Friedrich; Genealogie der Moral, 1887.

Pany, Thomas; Syrien-Krise und EU: Katastrophale Armut und Auswanderung als letzter Ausweg, 22. Februar 2024.

Perry, Markus; Understanding Organizational Culture: A Systems Theory Perspective, 2023.

Pfluger, Walter; Ronga – Ein Beispiel politischer Komplementarität, 1987.

Popper, Karl; The Open Society and its Enemies, 1945. Deutsche Ausgabe in 2 Bänden, „Die offene Gesellschaft und ihre Feinde", 1957 und 1958.

Prigogine, Ilya; Order through Fluctuation. Self-Organization and Social System, 1976.

Reid, Anna; Borderland, A Journey Through the History of the Ukraine, 2015.

Reinhard, Wolfgang; Die Unterwerfung der Welt: Globalgeschichte der europäischen Expansion 1414 – 2015, 2017.

Richard, Wilhelm; Weisheit des Ostens, von 1951.

Riemann, Fritz; Basic Forms of Fear. A depth psychological study, 1975.

Richter, Horst-Eberhard; Flüchten oder Standhalten, 2012.

Richter, Horst-Eberhard; Moral in Zeiten der Krise, Originalausgabe 2010.

Riegel, Tobias; Syrien – Die unendliche (Lügen-)Geschichte", 20. Februar 2020.

Riemann, Fritz; Grundformen der Angst. Eine tiefenpsychologische Studie. 10. überarbeitete und erweiterte Auflage, 1975.

Risk Management Network, Neue Ära der Großmachtkonflikte – Erosionsprozesse der geopolitischen Welt, am 7. Oktober 2019. https://www.risknet.de/themen/risknews/ero sionsprozesse-der-geopolitischen-welt/.

Rübel, Gerhard; Grundlagen der monetären Aussenwirtschaft, 2009.

Rügemer, Werner; Die Kapitalisten des 21. Jahrhunderts. Allgemeinverständliche Notizen zum Aufstieg der neuen Finanzakteure, 2018.

Rügemer, Werner; USA im Niedergang? – Aber in der EU so mächtig wie noch nie, Artikel im Online Magazin „Nachdenkseiten" vom 23. April 2019.

Sachs, Jeffry; Agenda der US-Aussenpolitik", am 20. Dezember 2023, auf dem Online Magazin Telepolis: https://www.telepolis.de/features/Kriegsdeba kel-und-viel-Geld-Die-geheime-Agendahinter-der-gescheiterten-US-Aussenpolitik-9584068.html?seite=all.

Sachs, Jeffry; https://www.jeffsachs.org/newspaper-articles/

Sakwa, Richard; Frontline Ukraine: Crisis in the Borderlands, 2022.

Sakwa, Richard; The Lost Peace: How the West Failed to prevent a Second Cold War, 2023.

Sakwa, Richard; Wir sind an der Beerdigung der alten Schule der Diplomatie, Interview vom 21. Mai 2024 in GlobalBridge.

Schmalz, Stefan und Ebenau, Mathias; Auf dem Sprung – Brasilien, Indien und China, 2011.

Schmalz, Stefan; Chinas neue Rolle im globalen Kapitalismus. in: Prokla 40 (4):483-503, 2015.

Schöllgen, Gregor; Das Zeitalter des Imperialismus (in Oldenbourg, Grundriss der Geschichte, Band 15), 2000.

Schuldt, Christian; Zeitalter der Krisen, Bundesverband „Energie, Wasser, Leben", 2021.

Sieren, Frank und Vossenkuhl, Josef, et al; "Zukunft? China! Wie die neue Supermacht unser Leben, unsere Politik, unsere Wirtschaft verändert", 2020.

Sieren, Frank; Shenzhen – Zukunft Made in China: Zwischen Kreativität und Kontrolle, 2021.

Sigrist, Christian; Regulierte Anarchie, 1967.

Sinn, Hans-Werner; Der Mythos vom Marshall-Plan, 03.02.2023.
https://www.hanswernersinn.de/de/marshallplan-brackmann-hb-03022023

Sinn, Hans-Werner;
https://www.hanswernersinn.de/de.

SIPRI – Stockholm International Peace Research Institute. SIPRI: https://www.sipri.org/databases/armstransfers.

Smith, Adam; Der Wohlstand der Nationen, Erstveröffentlichung 1776.

Spangler, David; The Flame of Incarnation, First edition, 2009.

Spengler, Oswald; Der Untergang des Abendlandes, erster Band 1918, zweiter Band 1922.
Spethmann, Dieter; Deutschland verschenkt seinen Wohlstand, am 19.01.2011 in der FAZ.

Spykman, Nicholas J.; Geography and Foreign Policy", published in The American Political Science Review, Vol. XXXII, Nos. 1 and 2, February and April 1938.

Steinbuch, Karl; Falsch programmiert – Über das Versagen unserer Gesellschaft in der Gegenwart und vor der Zukunft, 1968.

Steiner, Rudolf; Band GA 335 der Gesamtausgabe.

Steiner, Rudolf; Gesamtausgabe Band GA 185, Vorträge von 1918.

Stephanson, Anders; Manifest Destiny: American Expansionism and the Empire of Right, 1995.

Straubhaar, Thomas; Der Untergang ist abgesagt: Wider die Mythen des Demographischen Wandels, 2016.

Thomas, Anthony; Rhodes: the Race for Africa, 1997.

Tiger, Lionel und Fox, Robin; The Imperial Animal, 1976.

Todd, Emmanuel; La Défaite de l'Occident, von 2024.

Todd, Emmanuel; Weltmacht USA: ein Nachruf, 2003.

Tofler, Alvin ; Revolutionary Wealth, 2006.

Toynbee, Arnold J.; Essay aus dem Jahre 1934. "Things Not Foreseen at Paris; The Future in Retrospect".

Vidal, Gore; Perpetual War for Perpetual Peace: How we got to be so hated. American Imperialism, Book 1", 2002.

Wallerstein, Immanuel; Aufstieg und zukünftiger Niedergang des kapitalistischen Weltsystems. Zur Grundlegung vergleichender Analyse. In: Senghaas, Dieter (Hrsg.): Kapitalistische Weltökonomie. Kontroversen über ihren Ursprung und ihre Entwicklungsdynamik, 1979 und 1982.

Wallerstein, Immanuel; The Capitalist World-Economy, 1979.

Wang, Mingyuan; Why Have Repeated Efforts to Revitalize the Northeast Failed? – Rethinking the Twentieth Anniversary of the Strategy of Revitalizing the Old Industrial base.
https://www.readingthechinadream.com/wang-mingyuan-on-chinas-northeast.html.

Warburg, Paul M.; The Federal Reserve
System: its origin and growth; reflections and
recollections; 2 volumes, New York 1930.

Weidenhausen, Gerd; Buchbesprechung, in
Die Drei, Nr. 5.: Wolfgang Bittner, Die
Eroberung Europas durch die USA, 2015.

Wendt, Reinhard; Vom Kolonialismus zur
Globalisierung: Europa und die Welt seit 1500,
2016.

Wiener, Norbert; The Human Use of Human
Beings – Cybernetics and Society, 1950.

Wilhelm, Richard; Die Seele Chinas, 1925.

Willke, Hellmut; Global Governance, 2006.

Willke, Helmut; Atopia, 2001.

Wulf, Andrea; Alexander von Humboldt und
die Erfindung der Natur, deutsch 2016.

Wüthrich, Werner; Europäische Integration,
in dem Schweizer Magazin «Zeit-Fragen» von
2011 bis 2012.

Zeit-Fragen, Nr. 38, 2010: Studie zur „Geschichte der EU – Teil 1.

Zhao, Tingyang; Alles unter einem Himmel - Vergangenheit und Zukunft der Weltordnung, 2019.

ZHAO, Tingyang; All under Heaven: The Tianxia System for a Possible World Order, 2016.

Zürcher Kantonalbank, CBO, Census, OMB. https://www.zkb.ch/de/blog/anlegen/us-staatsverschuldung-rekordkurs.html.

Zürn, Michael; A Theory of Global Governance: Authority, Legitimacy and Contestation, 2018.